Peter Ro

Tolkien and Diversity

Proceedings of The Tolkien Society
Summer Seminar 2021

Edited by Will Sherwood

Contents

About the Peter Roe Memorial Fund   v
The Peter Roe Series   vii
Introduction
Will Sherwood   1

Desire of the ring: an Indian academic's adventures in her quest for the perilous realm
Sonali Arvind Chunodkar   7

Translation as a means of representation and diversity in Tolkien's scholarship and fandom
Martha Celis-Mendoza   29

La traducción como medio de representación y diversidad en los estudios sobre Tolkien entre la academia y los fans
Martha Celis-Mendoza   41

How Queer Atheists, Agnostics, and Animists Engage with Tolkien's Legendarium
Robin Anne Reid   52

Stars Less Strange: An Analysis of Fanfiction and Representation within the Tolkien Fan Community
Dawn Walls-Thumma   86

Hidden Visions: Iconographies of Alterity in Soviet Bloc Illustrations for *The Lord of the Rings*
Joel Merriner   107

"Something Mighty Queer": Destabilizing Cishetero Amatonormativity in the Works of Tolkien
Danna Petersen-Deeprose   119

The Invisible Other: Tolkien's Dwarf-Women and the 'Feminine Lack'
Sara Brown   140

The Lossoth: Indigeneity, Representation, and Antiracism
Nicholas Birns   154

"The Burnt Hand Teaches Most About Fire": Applying Trauma Exposure and Ecological Frameworks to Narratives of Displacement and Resettlement Across Elven Cultures in Tolkien's Middle-earth
V. Elizabeth King   167

The Problem of Pain: Portraying Physical Disability in the Fantasy of J.R.R. Tolkien
Clare Moore   191

About the contributors   201

About the Peter Roe Memorial Fund

The Tolkien Society's seminar proceedings and other booklets are typically published under the auspices of the Peter Roe Memorial Fund, a fund in the Society's accounts that commemorates a young member who died in a traffic accident. Peter Roe, a young and very talented person joined the Society in 1979, shortly after his sixteenth birthday. He had discovered Middle-earth some time earlier, and was so inspired by it that he even developed his own system of runes, similar to the Dwarvish Angerthas, but which utilised logical sound values, matching the logical shapes of the runes. Peter was also an accomplished cartographer, and his bedroom was covered with multi-coloured maps of the journeys of the fellowship, plans of Middle-earth, and other drawings.

Peter was also a creative writer in both poetry and prose—the subject being incorporated into his own *Dwarvish Chronicles*. He was so enthusiastic about having joined the Society that he had written a letter ordering all the available back issues, and was on his way to buy envelopes when he was hit by a speeding lorry outside his home.

Sometime later, Jonathan and Lester Simons (at that time Chairman and Membership Secretary respectively) visited Peter's parents to see his room and to look at the work on which he had spent so much care and attention in such a tragically short life. It was obvious that Peter had produced, and would have continued to produce, material of such a high standard as to make a complete booklet, with poetry, calligraphy, stories and cartography. The then committee set up a special account in honour of Peter, with the consent of his parents, which would be the source of finance for the Society's special publications. Over the years a number of members have made generous donations to the fund.

The first publication to be financed by the Peter Roe Memorial Fund was *Some Light on Middle-earth* by Edward Crawford, published in 1985. Subsequent publications have been composed from papers delivered at Tolkien Society workshops and seminars, talks from guest speakers at the Annual Dinner, and collections of the best articles from past issues of *Amon Hen*, the Society's bulletin.

Dwarvish Fragments, an unfinished tale by Peter, was printed in *Mallorn* 15 (September 1980). A standalone collection of Peter's creative endeavours is currently being prepared for publication.

The Peter Roe Series

I   Edward Crawford, *Some Light on Middle-earth*, Peter Roe Series, I (Pinner: The Tolkien Society, 1985)

II   *Leaves from the Tree: Tolkien's Short Fiction*, ed. by Trevor Reynolds, Peter Roe Series, II (London: The Tolkien Society, 1991)

III   *The First and Second Ages*, ed. by Trevor Reynolds, Peter Roe Series, III (London: The Tolkien Society, 1992; Edinburgh: Luna Press Publishing 2020)

IV   *Travel and Communication in Tolkien's Worlds*, ed. by Richard Crawshaw, Peter Roe Series, IV (Swindon: The Tolkien Society, 1996)

V   *Digging Potatoes, Growing Trees: Volume One*, ed. by Helen Armstrong, Peter Roe Series, V (Swindon: The Tolkien Society, 1997)

VI   *Digging Potatoes, Growing Trees: Volume Two*, ed. by Helen Armstrong, Peter Roe Series, VI (Telford: The Tolkien Society, 1998)

VII   *Tolkien, the Sea and Scandinavia*, ed. by Richard Crawshaw, Peter Roe Series, VII (Telford: The Tolkien Society, 1999)

VIII   *The Ways of Creative Mythologies*, ed. by Maria Kuteeva, 2 vols, Peter Roe Series, VIII (Telford: The Tolkien Society, 2000)

IX   *Tolkien: A Mythology for England?*, ed. by Richard Crawshaw, Peter Roe Series, IX (Telford: The Tolkien Society, 2000)

X   *The Best of Amon Hen: Part One*, ed. by Andrew Wells, Peter Roe Series, X (Telford: The Tolkien Society, 2000)

XI   *Digging Potatoes, Growing Trees: Volume Three*, ed.
            by Helen Armstrong, Peter Roe Series, XI (Telford:
            The Tolkien Society, 2001)

XII   Kenneth Chaij, *Sindarin Lexicon*, Peter Roe Series, XII
            (Telford: The Tolkien Society, 2001)

XIII   *The Best of Amon Hen: Part Two*, ed. by Andrew Wells,
            Peter Roe Series, XIII (Telford: The Tolkien Society,
            2002)

XIV   *Tolkien: Influenced and Influencing*, ed. by Matthew
            Vernon, Peter Roe Series, XIV (Telford: The Tolkien
            Society, 2005)

XV   *Freedom, Fate and Choice in Middle-earth*, ed. by
            Christopher Kreuzer, Peter Roe Series, XV (London:
            The Tolkien Society, 2012)

XVI   *Journeys & Destinations*, ed. by Ian Collier, Peter Roe
            Series, XVI (Wolverhampton: The Tolkien Society,
            2015)

XVII   *Death and Immortality in Middle-earth*, ed. by Daniel
            Helen, Peter Roe Series, XVII (Edinburgh: Luna Press
            Publishing, 2017)

XVIII   *Poetry and Song in the works of J.R.R. Tolkien*, ed.
            by Anna Milon, Peter Roe Series, XVIII (Edinburgh:
            Luna Press Publishing, 2018)

XIX   *Tolkien the Pagan? Reading Middle-earth through a
            spiritual lens*, ed. by Anna Milon, Peter Roe Series,
            XIX (Edinburgh: Luna Press Publishing, 2019).

XX   *Adapting Tolkien*, ed. by Will Sherwood, Peter Roe
            Series, XX (Ediburgh, Luna Press Publishing, 2021)

XXI   *Twenty-First Century Receptions of Tolkien*, ed. by
            Will Sherwood, Peter Roe Series, XXI (Edinburgh,
            Luna Press Publishing, 2022)

Abbreviations

A&I	*The Lay of Aotrou and Itroun*, ed. by Verlyn Flieger (London: HarperCollins, 2016)
Arthur	*The Fall of Arthur,* ed. by Christopher Tolkien (London: HarperCollins, 2013; Boston: Houghton Mifflin Harcourt, 2013)
AW	*Ancrene Wisse* (Oxford: Oxford University Press, 1962)
B&L	*Beren and Lúthien*, ed. by Christopher Tolkien (London: HarperCollins, 2017)
Beowulf	*Beowulf: A Translation and Commentary, together with Sellic Spell*, ed. by Christopher Tolkien (London: HarperCollins, 2014; Boston: Houghton Mifflin Harcourt, 2014)
Bombadil	*The Adventures of Tom Bombadil and other verses from the Red Book* (London: George Allen & Unwin, 1962; Boston: Houghton Mifflin, 1962)
CoH	*The Children of Húrin*, ed. by Christopher Tolkien (London: HarperCollins, 2007; Boston: Houghton Mifflin Harcourt, 2007)
Exodus	*The Old English Exodus*, ed. by Joan Turville-Petre (Oxford: Oxford University Press, 1982)
	Father Christmas Letters from Father Christmas, ed. by Baillie Tolkien (London: George Allen & Unwin, 1976; Boston: Houghton Mifflin, 1976)

FoG	*The Fall of Gondolin*, ed. by Christopher Tolkien (London: HarperCollins, 2018).
FR	*The Fellowship of the Ring*
Hobbit	*The Hobbit*
Jewels	*The War of the Jewels,* ed. by Christopher Tolkien (London: HarperCollins, 1994; Boston: Houghton Mifflin, 1994)
Kullervo	*The Story of Kullervo,* ed. by Verlyn Flieger (London: HarperCollins, 2015; Boston: Houghton Mifflin Harcourt, 2016)
Lays	*The Lays of Beleriand,* ed. by Christopher Tolkien (London: George Allen & Unwin, 1985; Boston: Houghton Mifflin, 1985)
Letters	*The Letters of J.R.R. Tolkien,* ed. by Humphrey Carpenter with the assistance of Christopher Tolkien (London: George Allen & Unwin, 1981; Boston: Houghton Mifflin, 1981)
Lost Road	*The Lost Road and Other Writings*, ed. by Christopher Tolkien (London: Unwin Hyman, 1987; Boston: Houghton Mifflin, 1987)
Lost Tales I	*The Book of Lost Tales, Part One,* ed. by Christopher Tolkien (London: George Allen & Unwin, 1983; Boston: Houghton Mifflin, 1984)
Lost Tales II	*The Book of Lost Tales, Part Two*, ed. by Christopher Tolkien (London: George Allen & Unwin, 1984; Boston: Houghton Mifflin, 1984)

Monsters	*The Monsters and the Critics and Other Essays* (London: George Allen & Unwin, 1983; Boston: Houghton Mifflin, 1984)
Morgoth	*Morgoth's Ring*, ed. by Christopher Tolkien (London: Geore, 1993; Boston: Houghton Mifflin, 1993)
OFS	*Tolkien On Fairy-stories*, ed. by Verlyn Flieger and Douglas A. Anderson (London: HarperCollins, 2008)
P&S	*Poems and Stories* (London: George Allen & Unwin, 1980; Boston: Houghton Mifflin, 1994)
Peoples	*The Peoples of Middle-earth*, ed. by Christopher Tolkien (London: HarperCollins, 1996; Boston: Houghton Mifflin, 1996)
Perilous Realm	*Tales from the Perilous Realm* (London: HarperCollins, 1997)
RK	*The Return of the King*
Silmarillion	*The Silmarillion*, ed. by Christopher Tolkien (London: George Allen & Unwin, 1977; Boston: Houghton Mifflin, 1977).
Sauron	*Sauron Defeated*, ed. by Christopher Tolkien (London: HarperCollins, 1992; Boston: Houghton Mifflin, 1992)
Secret Vice	*A Secret Vice: Tolkien on Invented Languages*, ed. by Dimitra Fimi and Andrew Higgins (London: HarperCollins, 2016)

Shadow	*The Return of the Shadow*, ed. by Christopher Tolkien (London: Unwin Hyman, 1988; Boston: Houghton Mifflin, 1988)
Shaping	*The Shaping of Middle-earth*, ed. by Christopher Tolkien (London: George Allen & Unwin, 1986; Boston: Houghton Mifflin, 1986)
S&G	*The Legend of Sigurd and Gudrún*, ed. by Christopher Tolkien (London: HarperCollins, 2009; Boston: Houghton Mifflin Harcourt, 2009)
TL	*Tree and Leaf*, 2nd edn (London: Unwin Hyman, 1988; Boston: Houghton Mifflin, 1989)
TT	*The Two Towers*
Treason	*The Treason of Isengard*, ed. by Christopher Tolkien (London: Unwin Hyman; Boston: Houghton Mifflin, 1989)
UT	*Unfinished Tales of Númenor and Middle-earth*, ed. by Christopher Tolkien (London: George Allen & Unwin, 1980; Boston: Houghton Mifflin, 1980)
War	*The War of the Ring*, ed. by Christopher Tolkien (London: Unwin Hyman, 1990; Boston: Houghton Mifflin, 1990)

Introduction

Will Sherwood

In *Twenty-First Century Tolkien* (2022), Nick Groom posits that "Middle-earth is teeming with diversity in races and species, as well as in flora and fauna – indeed, diversity is one of its characteristics," elucidating that the legendarium is a "quiet appreciation of language, landscape, diversity, modern heroism, failure, doubt and decline" (306-7). One aspect of J.R.R. Tolkien's writing that Groom stresses is the removal of the anthropocentric (non-Human) perspective; we experience Middle-earth through the words and eyes of Hobbits and Elves – it is, for example, through Gimli's paradoxical fear of the Paths of the Dead that we understand the terrors of Tolkien's subterranean world (322-3).

Tolkien's interest in alterity (the state of the other/otherness) has been theorised to partially stem from his own experiences as a Roman Catholic in a predominantly Protestant England (Vaccaro and Kisor 2017, 5). Moreover, his philological career highlights his fascination with diversity as he "delighted in the otherness of languages [...] emphasiz[ing] the importance of language to the identity of both peoples and individuals" (Dawson 2017, 186-7). For Tolkien, then, characters who "see through the veils of culturally-constructed binaries [...] are better for their expansive, even cosmopolitan awareness of their world's diversity," revealing the author's perspective on diversity's importance (Vaccaro and Kisor 2017, 5).

These points highlight one of the central truisms of Tolkien's sub-creation by depicting the innate strength of different peoples who unite to "triumph over what is predominantly a moral foe" (Fimi 2018). However, as Dimitra Fimi, a leading scholar in the field of Tolkien studies, has carefully laid out in her foundational and ground-breaking monograph *Tolkien, Race and Cultural History: From Fairies to Hobbits* (2009), Tolkien's racial prejudice is "linked to theological and spiritual factors," the medieval Greater Chain of Being, and "stereotypical ideas straight out of Victorian anthropology" (2009, 131-59). Therefore, individual examples of diversity in Middle-earth derive from disparate aspects of Tolkien's polymathic mindset. Although Janet Brennan Croft and Leslie A. Donovan's stellar collection *Perilous and Fair: Women in the Works and Life of J.R.R. Tolkien* (2015) rightly aims to "remedy perceptions that Tolkien's works are bereft of female characters, are colored by anti-feminist tendencies, and have yielded little serious academic work on women's issues" (2), readers still notice the marginalisation of female characters in Tolkien's works, leading to adaptations that seek to address the deficit (to varying success)[1] and female-centric fanfiction.[2]

This evinces that, as Verlyn Flieger poignantly reminds us, "everybody has their own private Tolkien" (2019, 9). Due to Tolkien's development as a writer, his continuously evolving legendarium, his views that adapted and changed over time, and every reader's own interpretation of the text they read, we concluded on *Tolkien and Diversity* as the theme for the 2021 Tolkien Society's Summer Seminar to provide a platform for

---

1. The decision to give Arwen greater agency in *The Lord of the Rings* trilogy (2001-2003) and the introduction of Tauriel in *The Hobbit* trilogy (2013-2015) being two examples.
2. As Dawn Walls-Thumma discusses in her contribution to this volume: 'Stars Less Strange: An Analysis of Fanfiction and Representation within the Tolkien Fan Community'.

voices that wished to build on existing scholarship or offer new, innovative insights into Tolkien's Middle-earth.[3] The seminar, which took place on Saturday 3rd and Sunday 4th July 2021, continued the Society's devotion to supplying the public with free access to research into Tolkien's life and works by being held solely online. The online platform supports my claim in *Twenty-first Century Receptions of Tolkien* (2022) that online/hybrid events allow for greater engagement from the Tolkien community as *Tolkien and Diversity* became the highest attended event in the history of the Society, welcoming over 700 delegates from around the globe for the two-day Zoom event (2).

Of the sixteen papers, ten are presented in this proceedings. Additionally, *Tolkien and Diversity* celebrates a new step in the direction of the Society's seminar proceedings in celebrating the multilingualism of the Tolkien community by inviting authors to publish papers in English and their first language. Sonali Arvind Chunodkar opens this volume by mapping the current state of Tolkien studies in India, building to an understanding of how film adaptations and translations have been received. Martha Celis-Mendoza addresses the impact of the lack of Tolkien translations in Mexico, posing the wider claim that there needs to be a greater dialectic relationship between languages to broaden Tolkien scholarship. Next, Robin Anne Reid provides part of her project on how atheists, agnostics,

---

3. Recall that the Orcs' origins underwent significant scrutiny, just as *The Hobbit*'s connection to the legendarium adapted between its publication in 1937 and its 'The Fifth Phase' in 1960 where he tried to "reconcile it to the later story in chronology, geography, and style" (Rateliff 2013, 765). Furthermore, although Tolkien (privately) declared in 1953 that *The Lord of the Rings* was a "fundamentally religious and Christian work" (*Letters*, Letter 142, 172), he later opined in 1967 (publicly) that it "was not a christian [sic] myth" (Resnick 1967, 43).

Animists, and those who are part of New Age movements interpret Tolkien's work, distributing parts of her survey across her paper and accompanying appendix.

The proceedings move on to Dawn Walls-Thumma's examination of the historical and current uses of fanfiction to address issues of representation in Tolkien's canon, drawing on Tolkien fanfiction surveys to consider whether and how these values have changed over twenty years of a significant online fanfiction fandom. Joel Merriner then introduces us to 1980s Russian, Polish, and Ukrainian illustrations of *The Lord of the Rings*, revealing the familiar yet alien styles of these original creations.

Danna Peterson-Deeprose follows with an intersectional analysis of Tolkien through a feminist and postmodern queer theory lens, examining how his depictions of characters, relationships, and ways of loving and existing destabilize contemporary cishetero amatonormative structures. Sara Brown invites us into the Dwarven realms, reading the 'invisibility' and marginalisation of Tolkien's female Dwarves through Julia Kristeva, Simone de Beauvoir, and Judith Butler.

The second half of the proceedings begins with Nicholas Birns's study of the meaningfulness of the Lossoth's momentary appearance in the legendarium, considering how they operate as an internal break upon Eurocentrism.

The penultimate paper by V. Elizabeth King reads the trauma exposure inherent in Middle-earth's refugee narratives and forced displacement, examining how they function differently across cultures within the legendarium and how those differences may impact reader experience. Clare Moore concludes the proceedings with an analysis of how Tolkien portrays pain in relationship to physical disability, focusing on the sustained but silenced pain of Frodo, Beren, Maedhros and Morgoth.

On behalf of the Tolkien Society, I would like to extend my deepest gratitude to the presenters of the Tolkien Society 2021 Summer Seminar, without whom the event would not have happened. I would also like to thank the Society's committee for their continued support and guidance in the planning and running of the event, and the publishing of this proceedings. Further, I wish to thank S.R. Westvik and Professor Craig Franson for their wisdom, support, and encouragement throughout 2021, and Professor Robin Anne Reid and Professor Yvette Kisor who sat on the paper panel and helped create the schedule. The publication itself is made possible by the generosity of the Peter Roe Memorial Fund, for which I am grateful.

To conclude I leave you with the final words of Fimi's monograph: "stepping into the road of Tolkien scholarship can be an adventure in its own right [...] with an open mind and meticulous work it can be a well-worth adventure" (2009, 203).

Bibliography

Croft, J.B., and Donovan, L.A., 'Introduction: Perilous and Fair, Ancient and Modern, Luminous and Powerful', in *Perilous and Fair: Women in the Works and Life of J.R.R. Tolkien*, ed. by Janet Brennan Croft and Leslie A. Donovan (Altedena: Mythopoeic Press, 2015), pp. 1-8.

Dawson, Diedre, 'Language and Alterity in Tolkien and Lévinas', in *Tolkien and Alterity*, ed. by Christopher Vaccaro and Yvette Kisor (Basingstoke: Palgrave Macmillian, 2017), pp. 183-204.

Fimi, Dimitra, *Tolkien, Race and Cultural History*, (Basingstoke: Palgrave Macmillan, 2009).
--- 'Was Tolkien really racist?', *The Conversation*, 6 December 2018.

Groom, Nick, *Twenty-First Century Tolkien*, (London: Atlantic Books, 2022).

Rateliff, J.D., *The History of the Hobbit*, (London: HarperCollins, 2013).

Resnik, Henry, 'An Interview with Tolkien', *Niekas*, 18 (1967), 37-47.

Sherwood, Will, 'Introduction', in *Twenty-first Century Receptions of Tolkien*, ed. by Will Sherwood (Edinburgh: Luna Press Publishing, 2022), pp. 4.

Tolkien. J.R.R., *The Letters of J.R.R. Tolkien*, ed. by Humphrey Carpenter with the assistance of Christopher Tolkien (London: HarperColllins, 2005).

Vaccaro, C., and Kisor, Y., 'Introduction', in *Tolkien and Alterity*, ed. by Christopher Vaccaro and Yvette Kisor (Basingstoke: Palgrave Macmillian, 2017), pp. 1-16.

Desire of the ring: an Indian academic's adventures in her quest for the perilous realm

Sonali Arvind Chunodkar

This paper presents, in an introductory manner, four aspects of my reading and study of J.R.R. Tolkien's fantasy fiction while being based in India. In the first section, I share some observations drawn from my experience of being a second-generation Tolkien researcher in Indian academia. This section offers an overview of the kind of research work that has been undertaken in India, while diagrammatically indicating the possible approaches to conducting any research and discussion on Tolkien's works in general. The second section outlines the basic types of knowledge that readers in general are expected to possess for engaging with and enjoying Tolkien's works. It hints at the interesting epistemic possibility of certain actual world flora and archaic words in Tolkien's works often being considered as uniquely fictional ones belonging only to his secondary world.

The third section offers a passing glimpse of the cultural and critical milieu grounding the popularity of Tolkien's works and their film adaptations in India. It notes their influence on the rise of English-language fantasy fiction in India. This section also includes some of the reasons for the lukewarm reception of the Marathi translation of *The Lord of the Rings* in particular. The final section attempts an intervention in the ongoing debates around Sam's described skin colour offering arguments against the more usual readerly interpretations of him being 'tanned' or 'mud-stained'.

1 - Far from the Door where it Began: On the Fellowship of Tolkien Researchers in India

What confronts one while studying Tolkien's fantasy fiction in a university in India is an awareness of the difficulty in accessing related useful scholarly publications and the restricted possibility of learning from established scholars in the area. This awareness has been aptly expressed in the following reminiscence by Aniket Jaaware, who wrote — to the best of my knowledge[1] — the first Ph.D. dissertation on Tolkien's fantasy fiction in India during the late 1980s:

> There was a time when I was seriously under the impression that I could study, for a research degree, the writings of the British novelist J.R.R. Tolkien [...] Working in what I am fond of calling the 'remote corners of western civilization', i.e., in Pune, there was only a remote possibility of my getting hold of writings on Tolkien's writings. So I thought I could work on some other author, say Graham Greene or Thomas Hardy [...] but I soon found out that I would have the same difficulty of accessing material, with only degrees of difference. So I thought I would work on some Indian author, who wrote in the 19th century. The same difficulty presented itself. In short, whether we like it or not, material is not as easily available to Indian researchers (unless they are situated in 'metropolitan' places — and even there, material is not always available).[2] (2001, 64)

1. The first mention of any Ph.D. dissertation on Tolkien, which is of Jaaware's 1989 dissertation, in currently accessible bibliographical records — such as the Association of Indian Universities' multi-volumed *Bibliography of Doctoral Dissertations: Social Sciences and Humanities* and INFLIBNET's Shodhganga website — appears in the 1991 volume of the former (see 1994, 198). I must caution that the information available through these sources may not be comprehensive; furthermore, these sources do not include any record of M.Phil. theses.
2. This difficulty is not restricted to researchers based in India.

He nonetheless continued working on his "risky project," which saw the light of day because of the support of his own supervisor and a few other then-faculty members who had in turn completed their own doctoral studies in the UK and the US (1989, i). He also acknowledged Christina Scull of The Tolkien Society and Rayner Unwin for coming to his proverbial rescue when it came to learning about and acquiring books by and about Tolkien for his research while visiting the UK (i).

Twenty-three years since then, my own endeavour to study Tolkien's works for a research degree was not as risky but still quite rare.[3] While there remained some academic distrust towards fantasy fiction at that time, I found much encouragement in the existence of scholarly work being produced by Anglo-American academics. More importantly, Jaaware's academic and teaching history became instrumental in conjuring institutional acceptance for my research projects.[4] My own introduction to Tolkien's works was facilitated by the ready availability of *The Hobbit* and *The Lord of the Rings* in bookstores and libraries in a metropolis like Mumbai. The marketing campaign surrounding Peter Jackson's trilogies since 2002 and their resultant popularity have ensured that several urban bookstores continue to house Tolkien's fictional and some non-fictional books.[5]

When it came to book-length scholarly publications on Tolkien, however, not much had changed since Jaaware's times. For instance, for my own research, I have often had to take recourse to online resources such as Google Books preview version and online retail websites like Flipkart and

---

3. The Shodhganga online repository currently displays at least four entries for Ph.D. dissertations on Tolkien for the intervening period (INFLIBNET).
4. Through his initiative, the Department of English at Savitribai Phule Pune University (formerly known as the University of Pune) had offered an optional course on 20th century fantasy fiction for M.A. students.
5. Jackson's *The Fellowship of the Ring* was first released in India in 2002.

Amazon.[6]   While affordable Kindle editions of select books started becoming available in the mid-2010s, print copies of most full-length scholarly books continue to remain out of bounds on a student's budget. Under such conditions, I have had to rely quite often on legally and ethically problematic websites that share e-copies of some of these scholarly works.

Despite Tolkien's own battle with Ace Books against book piracy, when it comes to scholarly works and areas like the Global South, any morally absolutist view against such reliance and any attempt at a similar call for "courtesy" would overlook the much larger inequalities of affordable access to research (Lobdell 2007, 391).[7] The appearance of open-access Tolkien research journals since the mid-2010s have nonetheless come some way towards enabling such access. The shift towards online seminars and conferences during the Covid-19 pandemic have also helped further realize the possibility of a global dialogue and research exchange, besides providing avenues for learning from established Tolkien scholars.

The limited access to published and archival material has obviously determined the research areas one could fruitfully engage with while remaining in places like India. In his Ph.D. dissertation, Jaaware walked a more theoretical path: borrowing select concepts from philosophical thinkers like Aristotle, Martin Heidegger, Roman Ingarden, and Hans-Georg Gadamer, he arrived at diagrammatic accounts of the causes, grounds, and necessary conditions for the 'being' of

6. These two e-commerce companies began their operations in India in 2007 and 2013, respectively.
7. These inequalities arise in part from the geographical location of relevant publishing houses in the US and Europe, the international implementation of and publishers' adherence to only these countries' copyright licensing laws, as well as the library funding priorities of inadequately funded Indian universities (see Reddy and Rakhecha 2021; cf. Bohannon 2016).

any novel or any other kind of work of art (1989). He relied on Tolkien's and Anthony Powell's respective novels to test the validity of his schemas. He also emphasized how his diagrams could help map most — if not all — of the possible approaches to studying or discussing any possible literary or other work of art (1989; 36, 44-6; see Diagram 1).[8]

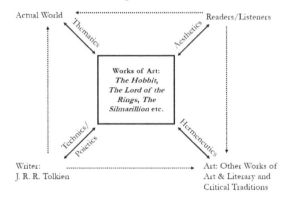

Diagram 1. A Map of Writer-, Reader-, and Work-focused Possible Approaches to Tolkien's Fantasy Fiction (adapted from Jaaware 1989; 23, 49)

8. Any research or discussion can be directed, for instance, toward the work of art in relation to the writer's artistic production and techniques (Writer–Technics/Poietics axis); to matters and materials pertaining to the actual world as well as its thematized textual representations (Actual World–Thematics axis); to artistic, critical traditions and conventions embodied in other works, genres, media, criticisms, and interpretations of art (Art–Hermeneutics axis); and to readers/listeners' response and reception (Reader/Listener–Aesthetics axis) (22-30, 35-6, 39-40). Such research or discussion can also be directed toward any combination of these axes: one can also consider the work of art in relation to, for example, the Actual World–Writer axis, Actual World–Thematics–Writer–Technics/Poietics–Art–Hermeneutics axes, Actual World–Thematics–Reader/Listener axes, Aesthetics–Reader/Listener–Art–Hermeneutics axes, Writer–Actual World–Thematics–Reader/Listener–Aesthetics axes, Writer–Technics/Poietics–Aesthetics–Reader/Listener axes, and so on. Jaaware cautions that any relation between the Writer and the Reader/Listener as such is necessarily mediated by the work of art (43).

Any worthwhile writer-focused research continues to be beyond our respective reach because of our geographical distance to Tolkien's as-yet unpublished writings and other archival material.[9] Reception-centric studies were quite restricted in scope during Jaaware's times; however, that is no longer the case as can be discerned from this very paper.[10] The research paths most taken have been those that focus on Tolkien's works in their relation to combinations of the Actual World–Thematics, Art–Hermeneutics, Aesthetics–Reader/Listener axes (see Diagram 1).[11] Studies on Tolkien's constructed languages, however, have remained sorely missing.

2 - Shadows of Other('s) Pasts: On (Indian) Readers Reading Tolkien

When it comes to the possibility of enjoying Tolkien's works, readers/listeners — Indian or otherwise — must possess some basic types of knowledge in order to achieve an 'adequate' — if not 'accurate' — cognition of Tolkien's works.[12] The

9. Writer-focused research includes tracing the various sources of influences on Tolkien's thinking and writing as well as the developmental history of his fictional and scholarly works, of his writing style(s), of his possible intentions, of his constructed languages, and so on. Such studies usually involve biographical, bibliographical, and archival research (Chunodkar 2014, 9).

10. Such research is usually concerned with public and academic reception of Tolkien's works, their adaptations in different media, their influence on popular culture, reading/listening experiences, and so on (Chunodkar 2014, 9).

11. In addition to the above-mentioned reader-centric approaches, these research axes also include thematic, comparative studies; those on rhetorical, narrative, and stylistic aspects; theoretical, philosophical, and ideological interpretations and applications; as well as linguistic research (Chunodkar 2014, 9). Almost all of the Ph.D. dissertations on Tolkien listed in the Shodhganga online repository can be accounted for along these axes (INFLIBNET).

12. The mere possession of these basic types of knowledge implies neither an

most fundamental of these is knowledge of the phonetic and/ or written form of the 'primary language(s)' of the works.[13] 'Primary languages' include not just English but any of the languages in which Tolkien's works have been translated. 'Secondary languages' are restricted to the passing appearances of words in other languages — constructed or otherwise — and related scripts.[14]

When it comes to semantic knowledge, which is another attendant basic type of knowledge, no reader/listener knows all the words belonging to the primary language in question nor their possible meanings. During one's first few engagements with Tolkien's works, such ignorance often results in curious (mis)understandings concerning the linguistic provenances of words, names, and phrases like Cob, Lob, Láthspell, Isengard, Gandalf, Beorn, Orthanc, Dwarrowdelf, Radagast, Attercop, and "Ferthu Théoden hál!" (Wilton 2002). Through resources like David Wilton's webpage (2002), one might come to realize that Tolkien uses words and phrases derived from Old and Middle English alongside his constructed languages. However, such words and phrases often end up being understood — at least upon first reading/listening — as belonging to his fictional constructed languages or, in some instances, as nonsensical.

Any reader/listener's desire for continued engagement with Tolkien's works, however, requires more than mere literacy and linguistic, semantic knowledge. What it also requires is

---

interest in the activity of reading nor the availability of leisure time for those who have an interest in reading.

13. One can enjoy Tolkien's works without being their reader per se: one can also listen to others' readings of the works. For a phenomenological consideration of the act of reading, see Chunodkar (2022).

14. In the case of Meena Kinikar's Marathi translation of *The Hobbit*, English — words of which appear in explanatory parentheses — operates as a secondary language (see 2011; 22, 73, 101).

prior acquaintance with at least some of the types of objects, actions, and experiences described in the works along with some of their various possible socio-cultural connotations and associations. These types of objects, actions, and experiences are usually of the everyday, mundane sort. However, at least some of these mundane objects — such as tea, apples, cabbages, potatoes, tobacco — are 'commonly known' only because of their historical introduction to other geographical areas, including England and Europe, by European trading expeditions, companies, and colonial rule. Indeed, an awareness of the very notion of colonization is called for on the part of a reader/listener of *The Lord of the Rings* ('At the Sign of the Prancing Pony', 149-50; 'The Window on the West', 671-2) and *The Silmarillion* (xxvi, 309-38; cf. *Peoples*, 422-38). As in the case of archaic words, different species of actual world flora that are not found in other regions or climates or are known to readers/listeners only by their local language names can similarly be taken to be the author's fictional inventions (cf. Orsini 2009, 207).

Another basic type of knowledge pertains to an awareness of the broad genre(s) of the works, which can be gleaned through their marketed genre classification, their physical location in a library or bookstore, recommendations from others, and so on. This awareness of genre(s) includes that of mytho-fantastic, folklore creatures like fairies, dragons, elves, dwarfs, and so on. These basic types of knowledge that Tolkien's works demand from any reader/listener are not unknown to most English-language readers/listeners in India today for two main reasons: 1) the continuing, constantly (re-)negotiated legacy of British colonial educational policies[15] and 2) the growth

---

15. The most quoted of these policies remains Thomas B. Macaulay's infamous, disparaging 'Minute' of 1835 (see Zastoupil and Moir 1999, 161-73).

of state-owned and private television broadcasting networks since the mid-1980s and early 1990s, respectively.[16] The latter played a crucial role in bringing fantasy and science fiction to urban middle-class viewers during those years: television programmes of the state-owned Doordarshan network during the late 1980s included, for instance, Disney's animated series, *Star Trek: The Original Series*, the dubbed Japanese series *Giant Robo*, and even Carl Sagan's popular science series *Cosmos: A Personal Voyage*.[17]

3 - Homeworld Bound: On Tolkien's Popularity in India

These years also saw a marked growth in the production of local television content, particularly in Hindi. Doordarshan, for instance, included locally produced programmes belonging to the broad genres of comedy, popular history, mythology, social drama, science fiction, and detective mysteries (see Aarav 2020; Kini 2018). These years also saw a few fantasy fiction series in Hindi. One of these was *Alif Laila* (1993-1997; One Thousand Nights), which was based on select stories from *The Arabian Nights*. Another television series, *Vikram aur Betaal* (1985-6; Vikram and Betaal), adapted stories from the *Vetala Panchavimshati* cycle (Twenty-five tales of Vetala).[18] This story cycle finds its oldest extant versions in two 11th century poetic

16. Mythological and fantastic, marvellous themes have been a constant feature of films produced in India since the early 1910s. For an indicative list of such films, albeit only those in Hindi, along with their posters, see Mike Barnum.

17. Jayant Narlikar, a well-known astrophysicist and science fiction novelist, introduced each episode of the Doordarshan telecast of *Cosmos*.

18. Richard F. Burton reworked some of these tales into *Vikram and the Vampire or, Tales of Hindu Devilry* (1870), while Arthur W. Ryder translated them as *Twenty-two Goblins* (1917). Both works were published in London.

compilations — Kshemendra's *Brihat Kathamanjari* (The Great Tale Collection) and Somadeva's *Kathasaritasagara* (The Ocean of Stories) (Das 2005, 102). These two Sanskrit compilations are held to be recensions of an even earlier though long-lost collection known as *Brihat Katha* (The Great Tale) by Gunadhya. This work is claimed to have been written in an 'unrespectable', now lost Prakrit language called *Paishachi*, which "literally means the language of the *pishachas* (the goblins)"[19] (Das 2005, 104).

Another popular television series in the 1990s was *Chandrakanta* (1994-1996), which was based on Devkinandan Khatri's popular four-part sword and sorcery novel of the same name (1888-1891).[20] Written in colloquial Hindustani, it got "thousands of readers" to learn the Khari Boli dialect in the Devanagari script thus "contributing successfully to the development of Hindi as the 'national' language and literature in late nineteenth century" (Orsini 2009, 198; Bharti 2016, 158).[21]

---

19. This word is also translated as 'ghouls', 'ghosts', and 'demons'. Andrew Ollett's 2014 article titled 'Ghosts from the Past: India's Undead Languages' offers a useful historical overview of the various scholarly opinions concerning the name as well as the possible, projected speakers of this mysterious language.

20. The novel's popularity led to the publication of sequels like the twenty four-part *Chandrakanta Santati* (1894-1905; Children of Chandrakanta) and the twenty one-part *Bhutnath* (1907-1913, 1915-1935), which was left unfinished upon Khatri's death in 1913 but was later completed by his son, Durgaprasad Khatri (see Orsini 2009, 200-1).

21. Meenakshi Mukherjee sheds further light on its popularity:

> Very soon *Chandrakanta* became a cult, and in ten years six editions of several thousand copies were sold out. When one takes into account the low percentage of literacy, limited reading habit and modest buying power of most Hindi readers of the period, this figure assumes impressiveness. The continuing popularity of *Chandrakanta* in the next three or four generations

Borrowing from Perso-Arabic and Urdu literary traditions of the *qissa* or *dastan*, Khatri's works are peopled with 'skillful' *aiyaar* and *aiyaara* and an almost 'technologically' explained *tilism* (see Bharti 2016, 154-7; Orsini 2009, 210-2; Roy 2016, 341-2).

Indeed, mythological and fantastic, marvellous elements have been an inescapable part of the Indian cultural milieu (see Das 1991 and 1995; Mukherjee 1985). It is therefore not surprising that Jackson's *The Lord of the Rings* trilogy became quite successful in India as well and generated much interest among viewers in Tolkien's own writings.[22] This interest also resulted in the publication of translated versions of *The Hobbit* and *The Lord of The Rings* in two languages — Bengali and Marathi. Aniruddha's Bengali translations, illustrated by Santi Prasad Chatterjee, are *Hobbit* (2011) and the first two volumes of *Sarbadhipoti Angti — Angtir Moitreesangha* (2012) and *Dui Minar* (2013).[23] Meena Kinikar translated *The Hobbit* (2011), while Mugdha Karnik translated the three volumes of *Swami Mudrikancha* (2015) — *Mudrikeche Sathidar*, *Te Don Manore*, and *Rajache Punaragaman* — into Marathi.

> can be seen in the fact that between 1891, the year of its first publication, and 1961, forty-five editions had come out, making the number of printed copies 1,800,000, even by a conservative estimate. (1985, 64)

For an overview of the problematic national, language, and religious identity politics that Khatri and his works were involved in, see Francesca Orsini (2009, 204-25) and Arora Bharti (2016). This work is also notable for its portrayal of strong female characters, specifically the *aiyaara* Chapala and Champa.
22. The *Harry Potter* films, the first of which released in 2002 in India, also played a significant role in popularizing English-language fantasy fiction.
23. The third volume, tentatively titled '*Moharajer Protyabartan*', has not yet been published, possibly because of copyright licensing issues (see Strelzyk; Chatterjee-Woolman 2013).

In the case of the Marathi translations, it seems that they have appealed mostly to a niche bilingual readership comprised of those who are already familiar with Jackson's adaptations and/or the novels in English. One of the reasons for the translation's lukewarm reception among Marathi readership in general is that they have had to compete with the already extant rich literary offerings in Marathi belonging to the genre of mythological fiction.[24] Furthermore, the Sanskritized literary style and vocabulary of *Swami Mudrikancha* in particular allows the work to feel completely at home in Marathi literary tradition as a 'descendant' of the *adbhut kadambari* (fantastic/marvellous novels) (see Das 1991, 201; Jaaware 2002).[25] For instance, the use of the word *mudrika* (signet or seal ring) rather than *angthi* (ring) can bring to the minds of Marathi readers the more well-known *mudrika* of the *Ramayana* tradition and of Kalidasa's *Shakuntala* through its various adaptations.

In light of what can be considered its linguistic, semantic, and genre naturalization, this translation also has to bear the brunt of historical criticism against works like the *adbhut kadambari*. This criticism is usually directed towards their recourse to fantastic, marvellous elements and archaic writing styles (see Das 1991; 201, 209). For instance, in her 1882 feminist tract '*Stri Purush Tulana*' (A Comparison between Women and Men), Tarabai Shinde offered an apt, pointed criticism of a few such

---

24. Examples of popular Marathi-language mythological fiction novels are V.S. Khandekar's *Yayati* (1959), Shivaji Sawant's *Mrityunjay* (1967) and *Yugandhar* (2002), and Ranjeet Desai's *Radheya* (1973).

25. Examples of these novels are Lakshman Moreshwar Halbe's *Muktamala* (1861) and *Ratnaprabha* (1878), Babaji Krishna Gokhale's *Raja Madan* (1865), and Naro Sadashiv Risbud's *Manjughosha* (1868). These works were characterized by "a highly Sanskritic style and rhetorical features of Sanskrit narratives" with "exciting incidents and moralization," "coincidences bordering on miracles," and "long and elaborate descriptions" (Das 1991, 197-8).

'escapist'[26] works for their dubious, unrealistic portrayal of female characters (Shinde and O'Hanlon 2000; 38-47, 114-7). *Dastan*-influenced works like *Chandrakanta* similarly suffered in light of the censure of, among others, the highly influential Munshi Premchand — who promoted the trend of social realism in Hindi literature — in his 1936 presidential address at the inaugural All India Progressive Writers' Conference (2011, 82). Such criticism shaped not just the literary tastes of contemporary and subsequent readership but also publishers' decisions.[27]

The popularity and economic success of Jackson's trilogy nonetheless facilitated a creative re-investment in the genre on the part of English-language novelists in India as well as movie and television producers in some Indian languages. Recent years have seen a marked rise in fantasy fiction novels in English in India's marketplace.[28] The influx of fantastic creatures and plots in the case of the already problematic genre of Indian television soap operas is quite troubling (see Virmani 2016). The last decade also saw the enormous success of the

26. Risbud, for instance, justifies his recourse to marvellous elements as an attempt to 'escape' from the boredom of uninteresting daily life (see Das 1991, 198). For V.K. Rajwade's views on escapism, epistemological powerlessness, and a sense of lack in connection with the 'origins' of the fantastic and of the human creative, imaginative impulse in his 1902 Marathi essay '*Kadambari*', see Milind Wakankar (2011, 97).

27. Bhalchandra Nemade, an influential Marathi author, professor of English, and a leading proponent of the social realism genre, was a more recent critic (see Sarang 2015).

28. These include Samit Basu's *The GameWorld Trilogy* (2004-2005), Indra Das's *The Devourers* (2015), Sukanya Venkatraghavan's *Dark Things* (2016), Tashan Mehta's *The Liar's Weave* (2017), and Shweta Taneja's Anantya Tantrist Mysteries series (2015-2018), in addition to the comparatively more popular but religio-politically fraught sub-genre of mythological fantasy fiction works like those of Ashok Banker and Amish Tripathi. Taneja offers some insight into why the readership of most of these fantasy and science fiction works remains restricted to India (2020).

two *Baahubali* films — *Baahubali: The Beginning* (2015)[29] and *Baahubali 2: The Conclusion* (2017). Greatly influenced by Hindu mythological epics, popular history, and even Jackson's *The Lord of the Rings*, they have been rightly criticized for their often-questionable treatment of female characters; casteism and religious, regional nationalism; as well as colourism and racism (see Kuttaiah 2017; Nair 2017).

4 - The Reader's Choices Concerning Mayor Samwise

Unlike *Baahubali*, which was not an adaptation, the popularity of Jackson's trilogies has helped cement the view that Tolkien restricts his positive characters to those who are White. However, one of the fundamental differences between the visual medium and the written one is the latter's essential, inescapable characteristic of never being descriptively complete (cf. *Monsters*, 159). Ingarden, a Polish phenomenologist, understood such descriptive incompleteness as "places of indeterminacy," which in turn call for the reader's own imaginative contributions:

> We find such a place of indeterminacy wherever it is impossible, on the basis of the sentences in the work, to say whether a certain object or objective situation has a certain attribute. If, for instance, the color of Consul Buddenbrook's eyes were not mentioned in *Buddenbrooks* (and I have not checked to see), then he would be completely undetermined in this respect. We know implicitly, through context and by the fact that he is a human being and has not lost his eyes, that his eyes are of some color; but we do not know which. There are

---

29. This film was nominated for the 42nd Saturn Award for Best Fantasy Film.

many analogous cases. I call the aspect or part of the portrayed object which is not specifically determined by the text a "place of indeterminacy." (1973, 50)

When it comes to imaginatively filling-in such "places of indeterminacy" in the case of Tolkien's works, it seems that we often fall back on the movies or other such illustrative representations of the characters.

Significantly, when it comes to describing colour, Tolkien is both general and specific. As far as generality in descriptions is concerned, Miriam Y. Miller observed that "Tolkien used a strangely limited palette — red, green, blue, black, gray, brown, yellow, and white (the last two are also referred to as gold and silver) — with very, very few exceptions" and that such "color words are used without modification; i.e., we see, again with very, very few exceptions, green, not pale green, or emerald green, or chartreuse" (1981, 3; see Agøy 2013). As far as colour specificity is concerned, Tolkien, unlike Ingarden's example, at least mentions the eye, hair, and skin colour of some of the principal characters and groups of peoples (see Agøy 2013, 55-8).

Much has already been written about the attendant racial implications and applications of Tolkien's descriptions of the facial features and skin colours of the different individuals and peoples of his world (see Fimi 2010; Young 2016; Reid 2017). Still, I would like to focus on the explicitly described skin colour of one particular positive character — that is, Samwise Gamgee — and that of "the most normal and representative variety" and "the most numerous" Hobbit "breed" of the Harfoots (*FR*, 'Prologue', 3). Through the discussion that follows, I hope we would be able to achieve that much-emphasized "recovery" from what Tolkien calls "the drab blur of triteness or familiarity

— from possessiveness" and "appropriation" (*Monsters*, 146).

Tolkien describes the Harfoots ("one with hairy-feet") as being "browner of skin" ('Nomenclature of *The Lord of the Rings*', 759; *FR*, 'Prologue', 3). He notes that by the time of the events described in *The Hobbit* and *The Lord of the Rings*, the "least numerous [...] northerly branch" of the Fallohides ("paleskin"[30]) had "mingled"[31] with both the Harfoots and the Stoors (*FR*, 'Prologue', 3-4; 'Nomenclature of *The Lord of the Rings*', 757). While Bilbo, Merry, and Pippin can be counted among those who have a "strong Fallohidish strain," Gandalf's description of Frodo as being "*taller than some and fairer than most*" marks him out as a Fallohide exemplar (*FR*, 'Prologue', 3-4; 'Strider', 166). On the other hand, he explicitly specifies Sam's skin colour as being "brown" (*TT*, 'The Stairs to Cirith Ungol', 714; *RK*, 'The Tower of Cirith Ungol', 915).[32]

---

30. Tolkien points out in his note on the word that "it is archaic since *fallow* 'pale, yellowish' is not now in use, except in *fallow deer*; and *hide* is no longer applied to human skin" ('Nomenclature of *The Lord of the Rings*', 757).

31. That this 'mingling' implies sexual and marital rather than merely socio-cultural mingling finds a parallel in his similar use of the word in a later text when describing the intermarriages between the "fair-haired men and women among the Folk of Bëor" who "had brown hair (going usually with brown eyes), and many were less fair in skin, some indeed being swarthy" and the "fair-skinned" people of Hador with their "flaxen or golden hair and blue-grey eyes" (*Peoples*, 307-8). That such 'mingling' took place among the hobbits as well is implied through Tolkien's note on Sam's sister Marigold in which he states that he used the name "because, containing gold and referring to a golden flower, it suggests that there was a 'Fallohide' strain (see *The L.R.* I 12 [2004 edn., p. 3; Prologue]) in Sam's family — which, increased by the favour of Galadriel, became notable in his children: especially *Elanor*, but also *Goldilocks*" ('Nomenclature of *The Lord of the Rings*', 760; see *RK*, Appendix B, 1096).

32. That the use of this word was not a mere oversight on Tolkien's part is strongly suggested by some of his earlier — albeit rejected — descriptions of the hobbits. For example, one finds him writing about the "browner-skinned" Bree hobbits and later even envisioning all hobbits as having "long clever

Unlike the ready acceptance of Frodo's skin colour, there has been cognitive resistance to accepting Sam's described skin colour. This resistance takes the form of attempts to explain it away as a "tan" that was acquired from "years of working outside" or conversely, as him being muddy or dirty because of his occupation as a gardener ('Samwise Gamgee' 2021). Both these non-textual, non-verisimilitudic readerly contributions assume that the other hobbits had spent most of their time indoors and that one can only have a tan if one 'works' outdoors. Accordingly, these explanations end up overlooking the absence of such 'tanned' or 'muddied' states where the other three hobbits are concerned despite all of them travelling mostly on foot towards Mordor.

However, Frodo is known to have gone "tramping all over the Shire" and often beyond from the year 3001 of the Third Age, which was the year of Bilbo's disappearance, till 3018, when he finally left Bag End (*FR*, 'The Shadow of the Past', 42; *RK*, Appendix B, 1090-1). Still, he remains "*fairer than most*" when he reaches Bree later that year (*FR*, 'Strider', 166). Even Aragorn, for all his "nearly thirty years" worth of travelling, including the time he spent "far into the East and deep into the South," manages to retain his "pale stern face" (*RK*, Appendix A, I, v, 1060; Appendix B, 1090; *FR*, 'At the Sign of the Prancing Pony', 156).[33]

---

brown fingers" (*Shadow*, 133-4, 312; see *Hobbit*, 'An Unexpected Party', 4). One also finds earlier versions of Strider being a "brown-faced hobbit" named Trotter (*Shadow*, 137-8, 350).

33. Such explanations also dismiss Tolkien's knowledge of the verb form "browned," which emphasizes the sense of being tanned and which he uses to describe the previously "very fair" Entwives: "For the Entwives were bent and browned by their labour; their hair parched by the sun to the hue of ripe corn and their cheeks like red apples" (*TT*, 'Treebeard', 476).

Rather, it would be more in keeping with Tolkien's explicit description of the three different but intermingled Hobbit "breeds" to see Sam as someone bearing a 'strong Harfoot strain' (*FR*, 'Prologue', 3; see 'Nomenclature of *The Lord of the Rings*', 760). To conclude, it is only when we recover his described skin colour, we become free to recognize the complicating and perhaps even promising implications and applications of Tolkien's Sam, a member of a lower social order in the Shire, becoming its elected mayor — however ceremonial the position — and thereby discover yet another aspect of Tolkien's still perilous realm.

Bibliography

Aarav, '101 Classic Old Doordarshan Serials from the 1980's and 90's', *ReelRundown*, 28 September 2020, <https://reelrundown.com/tv/Popular-Old-Doordarshan-Serials-And-How-to-Watch-Them-Now> [accessed 2 June 2021].

Agøy, Nils Ivar, 'Vague or Vivid? Descriptions in *The Lord of the Rings*', *Tolkien Studies*, 10.10 (2013), 49-67.

Association of Indian Universities, *Bibliography of Doctoral Dissertations: Social Sciences and Humanities 1991*, (New Delhi: Association of Indian Universities, 1994).

Barnum, Mike, *Cinema Jadoo*, blog, n.d., <https://cinemajadoo.wordpress.com> [accessed 2 June 2021].

Bharti, Arora, 'The Marvelously "Real" World of *Dastan*: Khatri's *Chandrakanta* and the Dynamics of Nationalism in Colonial India', *South Asian Review*, 37.2 (2016), 152-176 <https://doi.org/10.1080/02759527.2016.11933067>

Bohannon, John, 'Who's Downloading Pirated Papers? Everyone', *Science*, 352.6285 (2016), 508-512 <https://doi.org/10.1126/science.352.6285.508>

Chatterjee-Woolman, Suravi, 'Tolkien Translations: Tolkien in Bengali', *Tolkien Library*, 5 January 2013, <https://tolkienlibrary.com/press/1070-Tolkien-in-Bengali.php> [accessed 2 June 2021].

Chunodkar, Sonali Arvind, 'J.R.R. Tolkien's Narrators and their Mimetic Strategies: Toward a Cognitive Narratological Analysis of Secondary Belief', (unpublished MPhil thesis, University of Pune, 2014).
--- 'On the Absence of Intuitive Phantasy During the Act of Reading', in *Phenomenology of Phantasy and Emotions*, ed. by Thiemo Breyer, Marco Cavallaro, and Rodrigo Sandoval (Darmstadt: Wbg Academic, 2022), pp. 27-55.

Das, Sisir Kumar, 'The Novel', in *A History of Indian Literature 1800-1910: Western Impact: Indian Response*, (New Delhi: Sahitya Akademi, 1991), pp. 197-216.
--- 'Myths and Modern Indian Literature', in *A History of Indian Literature 1911-1956: Struggle for Freedom: Triumph and Tragedy*, (New Delhi: Sahitya Akademi, 1995), pp. 123-149.
--- 'The Prose Narratives and the Short Verses', in *A History of Indian Literature 500-1399: From Courtly to the Popular*, (New Delhi: Sahitya Akademi, 2005), pp. 92-117.

Fimi, Dimitra, *Tolkien, Race, and Cultural History: From Fairies to Hobbits*, (Basingstoke: Palgrave Macmillan, 2010).

INFLIBNET, *Shodhganga: A Reservoir of Indian Theses*, n.d., <https://shodhganga.inflibnet.ac.in/> [accessed 21 September 2021].

Ingarden, Roman, *The Cognition of the Literary Work of Art*, trans. by Ruth Ann Crowley and Kenneth R. Olson (Evanston: Northwestern University Press, 1973).

Jaaware, Aniket, 'A Cartography of the Novel: A Theory and a Methodology with Reference to J.R.R. Tolkien and Anthony Powell', (unpublished PhD dissertation, University of Poona, 1989).
--- *Simplifications: An Introduction to Structuralism and Post-Structuralism*, (New Delhi: Orient Longman, 2001).
--- 'Two Sentences: A Speculation of Genre in Early Marathi Novels', in *Early Novels in India*, ed. by Meenakshi Mukherjee (New Delhi: Sahitya Akademi, 2002), pp. 73-80.

Khatri, Devkinandan, *Chandrakanta*, (New Delhi: Sharda Prakashan, 2012).

Kini, Sashank, 'Pre-Liberalisation Children's Television in India', *Sahapedia*, 4 September 2018, <https://www.sahapedia.org/pre-liberalisation-children%E2%80%99s-television-india> [accessed 2 June 2021].

Kuttaiah, Pranav, 'The Problem with *Baahubali*'s Casteist, Supremacist Logic', *TheQuint*, 1 May 2017, <https://www.thequint.com/entertainment/cinema/rajamouli-post-caste-re-emerges-dont-forget-baahubali-casteism> [accessed 2 June 2021].

Lobdell, Jared, '*Lord of the Rings, The*: Success of', in *J.R.R. Tolkien Encyclopedia: Scholarship and Critical Assessment*, ed. by Michael D.C. Drout (New York: Routledge, 2007), pp. 390-392.

Miller, Miriam Y., 'The Green Sun: A Study of Color in J.R.R. Tolkien's *The Lord of the Rings*', *Mythlore*, 7.4 (1981), 3-11.

Mukherjee, Meenakshi, 'Recreating a Past: Fiction and Fantasy', in *Realism and Reality: The Novel and Society in India*, (Delhi: Oxford University Press, 1985), pp. 38-67.

Nair, Karthika S., 'A Feminist Reading of *Baahubali 2: The Conclusion*', *Feminism in India*, 5 May 2017, <https://feminisminindia.com/2017/05/05/baahubali-2-feminist-reading/> [accessed 2 June 2021].

Ollett, Andrew, 'Ghosts from the Past: India's Undead Languages', *The Indian Economic and Social History Review*, 51.4 (2014), 405-456 <https://doi.org/10.1177/0019464614550761>

Orsini, Francesca, '*Chandrakanta* and Early Hindi Fiction in Banaras', in *Print and Pleasure: Popular Literature and Entertaining Fictions in Colonial North India*, (Ranikhet: Permanent Black, 2009), pp. 198-225.

Premchand, Munshi, 'The Nature and Purpose of Literature', *Social Scientist*, 39.11/12 (2011), 82-86 <http://www.jstor.org/stable/24159090>

Reddy, Prashant, and Vishal Rakhecha, 'Sci-Hub Case: What India should do to Ensure that Academic Journals are Available at Fair Prices', *Scroll.in*, 11 February 2021, <https://scroll.in/article/985982/sci-hub-case-what-india-should-do-to-ensure-that-academic-journals-are-available-at-fair-prices> [accessed 2 June 2021].

Reid, Robin Anne, 'Race in Tolkien Studies: A Bibliographic Essay', in *Tolkien and Alterity*, ed. by Christopher Vaccaro and Yvette Kisor (Cham, Switzerland: Palgrave Macmillan, 2017), pp. 33-74.

Roy, Anjali Gera, 'Aja'ib, Ghar'aib, Tilismi Qisse, and Salman Rushdie's Tilismi Realism', *Comparative Literature Studies*, 53.2 (2016), 334-358 <https://doi.org/10.5325/complitstudies.53.2.0334>

Sarang, Vilas, 'The Perils of Nativism: An Essay by Vilas Sarang (1942-2015)', trans. by V.V. Badve, *Scroll.in*, 16 April 2015, <https://scroll.in/article/720798/the-perils-of-nativism-an-essay-by-vilas-sarang-1942-2015> [accessed 2 June 2021].

Shinde, Tarabai, and Rosalind O'Hanlon, *A Comparison between Women and Men: Tarabai Shinde and the Critique of Gender Relations in Colonial India* (New Delhi: Oxford University Press, 2000).

Strelzyk, Yvan, 'Bengali (India)', *Elrond's Library*, n.d., <http://www.elrondslibrary.fr/T_Bengali.html> [accessed 2 June 2021].

Taneja, Shweta, 'SF in India', *Locus Online*, 8 December 2020, <https://locusmag.com/2020/12/sf-in-india-by-shweta-taneja/> [accessed 2 June 2021].

Tolkien, J.R.R., *The Peoples of Middle-earth*, ed. by Christopher Tolkien (Boston: Houghton Mifflin, 1996).
--- 'On Fairy-Stories', in *The Monsters and the Critics and Other Essays*, ed. by Christopher Tolkien (London: HarperCollins, 1997), pp. 109-161.
--- *The Silmarillion*, ed. by Christopher Tolkien (London: HarperCollins, 1999).
--- *The Return of the Shadow*, ed. by Christopher Tolkien (Boston: Houghton Mifflin, 2000).
--- *The Hobbit or There and Back Again*, 2nd edn (Boston: Houghton Mifflin, 2001).
--- *The Lord of the Rings*, (London: HarperCollins, 2005).
--- *The Hobbit*, trans. by Meena Kinikar (Pune: Diamond Publications, 2011).
--- 'Nomenclature of *The Lord of the Rings*', in *The Lord of the Rings: A Reader's Companion*, ed. by Wayne G. Hammond and Christina Scull (London: HarperCollins, 2014) pp. 750-782.
--- *Swami Mudrikancha*, trans. by Mugdha Karnik, 3 vols (Pune: Diamond Publications, 2015).

'Samwise Gamgee', *Tolkien Gateway*, 23 May 2021, <http://tolkiengateway.net/wiki/Sam> [accessed 2 June 2021].

Virmani, Shruti, 'A Fly, a Daayan, a Nagin: The "Women" who Dominate Indian TV', *The Indian Express*, 29 May 2016, <https://indianexpress.com/article/entertainment/television/theres-a-fly-in-my-plot-sasural-simar-ka-naagin-yeh-hai-mohabbatein-2823539/> [accessed 2 June 2021].

Wakankar, Milind, 'The Function of Rajwade's Fantastic in Realist Novels: Reimagining Realism in Marathi Utopianism', *South Asian Review*, 32.1 (2011), 93-120 <https://doi.org/10.1080/02759527.2011.11932813>

Wilton, David, 'Old English in LoTR', *WordOrigins.org*, 1 December 2002, <https://www.wordorigins.org/harmless-drudge/old-english-in-lotr?rq=tolkien> [accessed 2 June 2021].

Young, Helen, *Race and Popular Fantasy Literature: Habits of Whiteness*, (New York: Routledge, 2016).

Zastoupil, Lynn, and Martin Moir, eds, *The Great Indian Education Debate: Documents Relating to the Orientalist-Anglicist Controversy, 1781-1843*, (London: Routledge, 1999), pp. 161-173.

Translation as a means of representation and diversity in Tolkien's scholarship and fandom

Martha Celis-Mendoza

In 2013, a debate began surrounding the publication of a new translation of *The Little Prince* by Raymundo Isidro Alavez into Hña Hñu, a native language of Mexico better known as Otomí, spoken by over 300,000 persons. As my compatriot and fellow translator Yásnaya Aguilar explains,[1] there were two conflicting opinions: some argued that it would have been better if the resources invested in the publication of *The Little Prince* in Hña Hñu had been put into publishing French or even Spanish translations of works in native Mexican languages, since the public has very little knowledge of literary works produced in those languages. Others argued that "the translation of *The Little Prince* was just a strategy for the colonization of thought through Western literature."[2] On the other hand, the advocates of this translation insisted on the advantages of having French literature translated into Hña Hñu and on the importance of continuing to translate more works into this language. Even

---

1. Yásnaya Aguilar is a writer, linguist, translator, researcher, and activist from Ayutla Mixe, in Oaxaca. She studied undergraduate courses in Spanish Language & Literature and received a Master's Degree in Linguistics at the National Autonomous University of Mexico. Her work focuses on the promotion and study of the linguistic diversity and the endangered indigenous languages in México.

2. "Hubo algunos más que incluso argumentaron que la traducción de *El principito* tan solo era una estrategia de colonización del pensamiento por medio de la literatura occidental" (Aguilar, 2013).

today, almost a decade later, both arguments are still strong. It is thanks to translation that a multitude of texts and authors have become available to a readership that otherwise would only have access to a single language, and thus, to a very limited worldview. In the following pages, I will discuss how translation can contribute to establish a wider and more diverse readership and scholarship.

Professor Tolkien held translation in the highest regard, and it is thanks to this art, craft or science, that his own works have been received by millions of readers in more than 50 languages. Naturally, the majority of the editions published in languages other than English are of *The Hobbit* and *The Lord of the Rings*. From *The Silmarillion* to *The Notion Club Papers*, *Beowulf* and *Sir Gawain*, the list of languages that the texts are translated into diminishes drastically. The same happens with Tolkien's own scholarship, which is rarely translated into other languages, based on the partial misconception that all scholars of an English-language author must be proficient enough, not only to read their work in the original language, but also all the major works of criticism around it. In Mexico, the official language is Spanish, the language of colonization, but there are over 60 Mexican languages, with over 300 dialectal variations and Tolkien's works do not exist in any of them; the same can be said about native African languages and so many others. Unfortunately, it poses a two-way challenge, since the works of fiction inspired by Tolkien's works, and specially academic research and criticism works written in other languages rarely reach English-speaking fandom and scholars.

In 1982 Glenn GoodKnight very thoroughly researched what translations were available at the time and published it in *Mythlore* with an updated version a decade later in 1992. As he declared in the introduction to his recount, his interest in

Tolkien's translations began just seven years earlier, when he visited Tolkien's daughter, Priscilla, during an academic visit to England. Coincidentally, he bought some books that had belonged to Tolkien at a charity event. He acquired many of the translations and continued his quest to collect translations of Tolkien's works via Carpenter's biography and contacted many foreign publishers, as well as Arden Smith, author of the column "Tolkien in Translation" in *Vinyar Tengwar*, Wayne Hammond and many other informants. The foundational research by GoodKnight shows that, at the time, Tolkien's works had been translated into over 30 languages. Naturally, the most translated work was *The Hobbit*, but even now in 2022, some of the lesser-known works remain untranslated into so many languages.

After his narrative introduction, GoodKnight offers an all-encompassing list, at the time of its publication, of the different languages that included foreign renditions of Tolkien's works. GoodKnight mentions that, at the time:

> *The Hobbit* has been translated into thirty-one languages; *The Lord of the Rings* into twenty. Twenty-nine of these languages are European (or in the case of Esperanto, European-based). This should not be surprising since his works, especially The Hobbit, have elements with which peoples from the Germanic, Scandinavian, Slavicand Romance traditions can culturally relate. His mythology is a certain distillation of many European elements, and is clearly not derived solely from English traditions. (GoodKnight, 1992, 69)

He shows that sometimes the most famous works, *The Lord of the Rings*, and especially, *The Hobbit*, had been rendered at the time into two or more different versions. As stated in his study, at the time most of the published translations dated back to the late sixties and seventies. The table he designed is very eloquent, as it shows, at first sight, how only a handful of works had been translated into more than ten languages (*The Hobbit, The Lord of the Rings, Farmer Giles of Ham, The Smith of Wootton Major* and *The Silmarillion*), and how only a handful of languages included over a dozen different translated works (Swedish, Dutch, German, Italian, and Spanish).

Table of First Date of Publication

	English	Swedish	Dutch	German	Polish	Portuguese	Spanish	Japanese	Italian	Afrikaans	Danish	Hebrew	French	Norwegian	Czech	Finnish	Slovak	Bulgarian	Hungarian	Rumanian	Serbo-Croat	Russian	Estonian	Indonesian	Greek	Icelandic	Catalan	Armenian	Ukrainian	Moldavian	Faeroese	Esperanto	Latvian
Hobbit	37	47	60	57	60	62	64	65	73		69	76	69	72	73	73	73	75	75	75	75	76	77	78	78	78	83	84	85	87	90	91	91
LotR	54	59	56	69	61	74	77	72	67		68	79	72	73	90	73		90	81		81	82			88		86						
Giles	49	61	71	70	62	86	81	75	75		89	68	74	80	90	78		88			86	86			80		79	88					
Tom	62	72	74	84		86		75	80		89	84	75																				
Smith	67	72	68	79	80	86	81	75	76	68	85	83	74		90	83					84	87					88						
Tree	64	72	77	82					76		87	92	74									91											
Niggle	45		71	79		86	81	75							90							80											
Fairy	45			84					73																								
Beo	37	75		84																													
E&W	63	75																															
Home	53	80							76																								
Silma	77	79	78	79	85	84	84	82	78		78	90	78		79												◊						
Father	76	76	76	78			82	76	80				77																				
Pref	40	75																															
Tales	80	82	81	83		85	88		81			88										86											
Letters	81		83	91									90																				
Appx		80	80	81		87																											
Bliss	83		83	83		87			84		83				◊																		
Vice	84		84																														
LT1	84	◊		86			90		86																								
LT2	84	◊		87			90		87																								
Pict									89																								
Bilbo	90			91																													

underlined = printed together with other titles

◊ = the book exists but publication date is either not known or verified

italic = year of publication in doubt

(GoodKnight 1992, 62)

During my visit to the Tolkien collection at Marquette University in 2011, I was drawn towards the Special Collections of Raynor Memorial Libraries. At the time, Tolkien's works had been translated into about 50 languages. The earliest one dates back to 1947 with the Swedish translation of *The Hobbit*; many translations (mainly of *The Hobbit* and *The Lord of the Rings*) were undertaken during the 60s and 70s. GoodKnight mentions the Index Translationum, published by UNESCO, as one of the sources he used in his research, although he found it partly unreliable nor all-encompassing. Although I agree with GoodKnight, I think it is an invaluable starting point when conducting research in relation to the different translations of any given text. Unfortunately, due to the pandemic, the UNESCO and all related offices are naturally focusing on more pressing matters and the site is currently in a suspended state. It would be important for scholars to maintain an up-to-date database that accounts for every available translation of Tolkien's works into different languages and dialect variants, as well as all relevant information regarding the translators and publishing houses, just as GoodKnight did at the time.

The first translation of *The Hobbit* into Spanish was not the 1982 Manuel Figueroa edition for Minotauro that everyone in Spanish-speaking countries is familiar with, but *El Hobito* (1964) by Argentine translator Teresa Sánchez Cuevas. According to translation scholar Jorge Fondebrider, echoing a famous maxim, the classics must be retranslated every ten to fifteen years.[3] There is therefore space for a much needed new Spanish translation, either to Castilian Spanish or, preferably, to one of the many Latin American dialect variants, since the semantic

---

3. "La lengua cambia y, como la lengua cambia, cambian las modas de traducción [...] se supone que cada diez o quince años los clásicos deben ser retraducidos" ("Corazón de tinieblas", 2021).

difference between those variants is often greater than the one that exists between variants of other languages, especially if we take into consideration how orality is represented in works of literature which include a hybrid component. Professor Mark Hooker explains that those translators who embark in producing versions of Tolkien's works "should be conscious of the hybrid nature of Tolkien's text and attempt to replicate it" (2004).[4]

Another aspect of the same conflict is that many works *by* Tolkien, including very recent publications, have been translated into many major European and Asian languages, but unfortunately that is not the case with most works *about* Tolkien, and that poses a two-way problem: research written in English is not reaching many scholars who are only speakers of other languages, and, probably more serious, almost no research that is being produced by scholars of other languages is reaching English-speaking audiences if it is not produced in English, in both cases this is due to the lack of translations. This is evident in Spanish where one of the few works that have been translated is John Garth's books, *Tolkien y la Gran Guerra* and *Los mundos de JRR Tolkien*, both published by Minotauro and translated by Dr. Martin Simonson and Dr. Eduardo Segura. Both translators have a well-earned reputation as scholars, and both have also been involved in the translation project of Tolkien's works like

---

4. "Translators translating Tolkien's 'translation' should be conscious of the hybrid nature of Tolkien's text and attempt to replicate it. "Hybrid texts allow the introduction into a target culture of hitherto unknown and/or socially unacceptable/unaccepted concepts through a medium which, by its non-conformity to social/stylistic conventions and norms, proclaims the otherness of its origin and thereby legitimizes its right to be heard. There is freedom of expression which is unhindered by said conventions," say Schäffner and Adab in their "The Concept of the Hybrid Text in Translation." Translators who ignore the hybrid nature of Tolkien's text are rejecting the legitimate claim of the otherness of his text to be heard." (Hooker, 2004).

Beren y Lúthien and *La historia de Kullervo*, also published by Minotauro.[5] While not intending to discredit Garth's scholarship, it is clear that the ongoing relationship between the translators and the publishing house, as well as the translators' solid academic reputation might explain, at least partially, why these works have been translated into Spanish while dozens of other works which are staple in Tolkien Studies have not.

When it comes to considering how Spanish scholarship has been translated, a clear example is *Uncle Curro* by José Manuel Ferrández Bru (2018), which has examined Tolkien's connection to Spain via Fr. Francis Morgan. The scholarly reception of *Tío Curro* has been very positive; definitely a well-deserved feat, that has been partly due to the good reviews (including John Garth, who wrote the preface for the English edition), its availability in English, and it author's presence in academic circles through publications in spaces such as *Mallorn* and *Tolkien Studies* (2018).[6] Further, when I asked Dr. Holly Ordway, author of *Tolkien's Modern Reading* (2021),

---

5. This publishing house has published the translation into Spanish of Humphrey Carpenter's famous biography of Tolkien; Wayne Hammond's *El arte de El Señor de los Anillos* and *El arte de El Hobbit*; Catherine Mcilwaine's two volumes related to the 2018 exhibition *Tolkien Maker of Middle-earth* at the Bodleian Library; Alan Lee's *The Lord of the Rings Sketchbook*; John Howe's *A Middle-earth Traveler: Sketches from Bag End to Mordor*; four books by David Day, as well as a couple of cooking and coloring books. All of these works are translations from texts written originally in English; sadly, it is not a surprise that there are no books in their Tolkien catalogue translated from other languages yet.

6. Other research by Ferrández Bru includes "Wingless fluttering: Some Personal Connections in Tolkien's Formative Years" in *Tolkien Studies: An Annual Scholarly Review*. Vol. 8.; "J.R.R. Tolkien's 'second father' Fr. Francis Morgan and other non-canonical influences", in *The Return of the Ring*, Luna Press Publishing, 2012; and "J. R. R. Tolkien and the Spanish Civil War", in *Mallorn*, no. 51, May 2011, pp. 16-9, https://journals.tolkiensociety.org/mallorn/article/view/78.

whether she had identified any Spanish language writers that she could claim that Tolkien had read, she referred me to Ferrández Bru for further information. This shows how his work has permeated English-speaking Tolkien scholarship thanks to the presence of English translation.[7]

If this is the case of scholarly work, can we imagine what happens to the contributions of fandom all around the world in so many different languages, many of them worthy of recognition, whether for their quality or for their impact? Lawrence Venuti has repeatedly stated that to much of the readership on a global scale the only material available is the one that is produced or translated into English (Venuti 1992, 5-6 *passim*). Naturally the work of fans can hardly be translated if it is not thanks to collaborative projects by non-professional translators to whom the public owes so much (Evans 2019, 179; McDonough Dolmaya 2019, 127). In his work *Translation, Rewriting and the Manipulation of Literary Fame*, André Lefevere has referred to the reasons why some words can reach a wider readership thanks to translation, identifying some of the factors that have an influence upon the decisions behind which works are translated and which are not (1992, 26-9 *passim*). Similarly, Robin Reid and Michael Elam have discussed how Tolkien's legacy is authorized by his readers:

> While no one can force in what ways Tolkien's works are reshaped and retold, no one would deny the impulse to judge

---

7. That is unfortunately not the case of many Spanish-speaking scholars, as well as those of other languages, who have, until very recently, been very scarcely represented, and that mainly thanks to conferences and seminars like those organized by the Tolkien Society or the Mythopoetic Society. That is the case, for example of Pedro Angeles-Ruiz's article published in the proceedings of the 2005 Tolkien Society, the volume *The Ring Goes Ever On* (I would like to thank Dr. Laura Michel for pointing me to it).

such reshapings and retellings in terms of authenticity—
whether they maintain fidelity to the originals. Who, then,
defines and authorizes such fidelity? Is it possible even to
authorize Tolkien at all? Perhaps, though, asking such questions
assumes artistic merit similar to other English language works
that repeatedly serve as sources for adaptation (*Beowulf, The
Canterbury Tales*, the dramas of Shakespeare, etc.). That
Tolkien's works are so widely and variously adapted by so
many, and in many cases very passionately, suggests their
intrinsic importance, so much so that one needn't be alarmed
at adaptations which seem to run far afield from whatever the
sources seem to contain or perform. (Reid & Elam 2016, 2)

The amount of criticism derived from any work of art, as
well as the different creative pieces inspired by it, are proof
of its relevance at a certain stage in history; in this case, also
of its artistic value. The multicited Tolkien quote from letter
130 to Milton Wadman has been put forward as a permit from
Tolkien himself for producing other works that originate in
his legendarium. Notwithstanding, great works of art cannot
determine how they are received by the public once they
have left the pen and the hands of the writer, just as much as
academies cannot regulate how the different peoples are going
to adopt, and adapt, a language. Language is a living organism
in constant evolution, and this evolution depends on the users of
the language, on the peoples who speak it and transform it; the
same can be said about masterpieces: the way they evolve will
depend not only on the artist, the sub-creator, in the sender's
end of the communication's model, but also on the public, the
readers, in the receiver's end.

In the aforementioned text, Lefevere refers to the impact
of anthologies upon deciding which works are more likely to

survive: "The process resulting in the acceptance or rejection, canonization or non.canonization of literary works is dominated [...] by very concrete factors [...] such as power, ideology, institution, and manipulation [...] [R]ewriting in all its forms occupies a dominant position among [such] concrete factors" (1992, 2). Reid and Elam analyze the evolution of those works selected by Zimbardo and Isaacs in their different anthologies, where they refer to the "commonly accepted recognition of *The Lord of the Rings* as a masterwork, a goal achieved not [only] by the merits of the work itself but [...] in part due to the more than fifty years of academic scholarship, which is why the necessity to expand Tolkien studies to include work on the adaptations and by scholars trained in a wider range of isciplines is important to note" (2016, 6).

During the 2021 Summer Seminar organized by the Tolkien Society, several presentations focused on the need for a greater presence of many underrepresented minority groups, among them, the speakers of languages other than English. The labor of public institutions, publishing houses and associations in support of offering more visibility to those groups is of the greatest importance, which is why this year's Seminar was so important. The existence of a language implies the existence of a unique set of concepts and an entirely distinct worldview. Like in the case of *The Little Prince*, the values of Tolkien's work, both ethic and aesthetic, artistic and for everyday life application, will bear a different fruit in speakers of Hña Hñu in Mexico, from that in speakers of Inuktikut, the language of the Inuit, and their appreciation and scholarly analysis will enrich the soil where they are transplanted.

Bibliography

Aguilar, Yasnaya, '¿Traducir "a" lenguas indígenas o "de" lenguas indígenas?', in *Este País*, 14 February 2013, <https://archivo.estepais. com/site/2013/%C2%BFtraducir-%E2%80%9Ca%E2%80%9D-lenguas-indigenas-o-%E2%80%9Cde%E2%80%9D-lenguas-indigenas/comment-page-1/>

'Corazón de las tinieblas: el clásico de Conrad regresa en una traducción moderna y erudita', interview with Jorge Fondebrider (2021), <https://www. infobae.com/grandes-libros/2021/04/17/corazon-de-las-tinieblas-el-clasico-de-conrad-regresa-en-una-traduccion-moderna-y-erudita/>

Evans, Jonathan, 'Fan translation', in *Routledge Encyclopedia of Translation Studies*, (London: Routledge, 2019).

Ferrández Bru, José Manuel, *"Uncle Curro". J.R.R. Tolkien's Spanish Connection*, (Edinburgh: Luna Press Publishing, 2018).

Garth, John, *Tolkien y la Gran Guerra* (translated by Eduardo Segura and Martin Simonson Barcelona: Minotauro, 2014).
--- *Los mundos de JRR Tolkien* (translated by Martin Simonson, Barcelona: Minotauro, 2021).

GoodKnight, Glen, 'J.R.R. Tolkien in Translation', *Mythlore*, 18.3 (1992), 61-69.

Hooker, Mark T., 'Tolkien in Chinese', *Translation Journal*, 8.3 (2004). <https://translationjournal.net/journal/29tolkien.htm>

Lefevere, André, *Translation, Rewriting and the Manipulation of Literary Fame*, (London: Routledge, 1992).

Evans, Jonathan, 'Fan translation', in *Routledge Encyclopedia of Translation Studies*, (London: Routledge, 2019).

McDonough Dolmaya, Julie, 'Crowdsourced translation', in *Routledge Encyclopedia of Translation Studies*, (London: Routledge, 2019).

Ordway, Holly, *Tolkien's Modern Reading: Middle-earth Beyond the Middle Ages*, (Park Ridge: Word on Fire Academic, 2021).

Reid, Robin A. and Elam, Michael D. 'Authorizing Tolkien: Control, Adaptation, and Dissemination of J.R.R. Tolkien's Works,' *Journal of Tolkien Research*, 3.3 (2016). <http://scholar.valpo.edu/journaloftolkienresearch/vol3/iss3/1>

Tolkien, J.R.R., *Beren y Lúthien* (translated by Martin Simonson, Barcelona: Minotauro, 2016).
--- *La historia de Kullervo*, (translated by Martin Simonson, Barcelona: Minotauro, 2018).

Venuti, Lawrence, *Rethinking Translation: Discourse, Subjectivity, Ideology*, (London: Routledge, 1992).

La traducción como medio de representación y diversidad en los estudios sobre Tolkien entre la academia y los fans

Martha Celis-Mendoza

En 2013, surgió un debate en torno a la publicación de una nueva traducción de *El Principito* de Raymundo Isidro Alavez al hña hñu, una lengua originaria de México más conocida como otomí, hablada por más de 300,000 personas. Como explica mi compatriota y colega traductora Yásnaya Aguilar,[1] abía dos opiniones encontradas: unos argumentaban que hubiera sido mejor que los recursos invertidos en la publicación de *El Principito* al hña hñu se hubieran destinado a publicar traducciones al francés o incluso al español de obras en lenguas originarias mexicanas, ya que el público tiene muy poca información acerca de las obras literarias escritas en dichas lenguas. Otros argumentaron que "la traducción de *El Principito* tan solo era una estrategia de colonización del pensamiento por medio de la literatura occidental" Por otro lado, los defensores de esta traducción insistían en las ventajas de contar con literatura francesa traducida al hña hñu y en la importancia de seguir traduciendo más obras a esta lengua (Aguilar, 2013). Aún hoy, casi una década después, ambos

---

1. Yásnaya Aguilar es escritora, lingüista, traductora, investigadora y activista de Ayutla Mixe, Oaxaca. Estudió la licenciatura en Lengua y Literatura Hispánicas y la maestría en Lingüística en la Universidad Nacional Autónoma de México. Su trabajo se centra en la promoción y el estudio de la diversidad lingüística y las lenguas indígenas en peligro de extinción en México.

argumentos siguen teniendo fuerza. Gracias a la traducción, multitud de textos y autores han llegado a un público que, de otro modo, sólo tendría acceso a una única lengua y, por tanto, a una visión del mundo muy limitada. El profesor Tolkien tenía un gran aprecio por la labor de la traducción, y es precisamente gracias a este oficio, arte, o ciencia, que sus propias obras han sido recibidas por millones de lectores en diferentes idiomas. En las páginas que siguen trataré de analizar cómo puede contribuir la traducción a establecer una comunidad más amplia y diversa de lectores y de estudiosos.

Gracias a las traducciones, las obras de J.R.R. Tolkien han llegado a millones de lectores en más de 50 idiomas. Naturalmente, la mayoría de las ediciones publicadas en lenguas distintas al inglés son las de *El Hobbit* y *El Señor de los Anillos*. La lista de lenguas a las que se han traducido otros de sus textos, desde *El Silmarillion* a *The Notion Club Papers*, *Beowulf* y *Sir Gawain*, se reduce de manera notable. Lo mismo ocurre con los estudios académicos Tolkien, que muy rara vez se han traducido a otros idiomas, con base en la idea errónea de que todos los estudiosos de un autor en lengua inglesa deben ser lo suficientemente competentes, no sólo para leer su obra en el idioma original, sino también todas las obras importantes de la crítica en torno a ella. En México, el idioma oficial es el español, la lengua de la colonización, pero existen más de 60 lenguas mexicanas, con más de 300 variaciones dialectales, y lamentablemente no existen traducciones de las obras de Tolkien a ninguno de ellos; lo mismo puede decirse de lenguas originarias africanas y tantas otras. Desgraciadamente, se trata de un reto que presenta dos vertientes, ya que las obras de ficción inspiradas en la obra de Tolkien y, sobre todo, los trabajos de investigación y crítica académica escritos en otras lenguas rara vez llegan a los fans o a los estudiosos de habla inglesa.

En 1982 Glenn GoodKnight investigó muy a fondo qué traducciones estaban disponibles en aquel momento, y lo publicó en *Mythlore*, donde también ofreció una versión actualizada una década más tarde, en 1992 . Como declara en la introducción de su artículo, su interés por las traducciones de Tolkien había comenzado sólo siete años antes, cuando visitó a la hija de Tolkien, Priscilla, durante una visita académica a Inglaterra. Casualmente, compró algunos libros que habían pertenecido a Tolkien en una venta de beneficencia. Adquirió muchas de las traducciones y continuó su búsqueda para recopilar traducciones de las obras de Tolkien gracias a la biografía de Carpenter y estableció contacto con varios editores extranjeros, así como con Arden Smith, autor de la columna "Tolkien in Translation" en *Vinyar Tengwar*, Wayne Hammond y muchos otros informantes. La investigación fundacional de GoodKnight señala que, en aquel momento, las obras de Tolkien se habían traducido a más de 30 idiomas. Naturalmente, la obra más traducida fue *El Hobbit*, pero incluso ahora, en 2022, algunas de las obras menos conocidas siguen sin traducirse a un sinnúmero de idiomas.

Tras su introducción narrativa, GoodKnight ofrece una lista exhaustiva, en el momento de su publicación, de los distintos idiomas en los que se contaba con versiones de las obras de Tolkien. GoodKnight menciona que, en aquella época:

El Hobbit se ha traducido a treinta y un idiomas; *El Señor de los Anillos*, a veinte. Veintinueve de estas lenguas son europeas (o, en el caso del esperanto, de base europea). Esto no debe sorprender, ya que sus obras, especialmente *El Hobbit*, tienen elementos con los que los pueblos de tradición germánica, escandinava, eslava y románica pueden relacionarse culturalmente. Su mitología es una cierta destilación de muchos elementos europeos, y está claro que no deriva únicamente de las tradiciones inglesas. (GoodKnight, 1992, 69)

GoodKnight apunta que, en ocasiones, las obras más famosas como *El Señor de los Anillos* y sobre todo *El Hobbit*, habían sido traducidas en su momento en dos o más versiones diferentes. Como afirma en su estudio, en aquella época la mayoría de las traducciones publicadas provenían de finales de los años sesenta y de la decada de los setenta. La tabla que diseñó es muy clara, ya que muestra, a primera vista, cómo sólo un puñado de obras habían sido traducidas en ese momento a más de diez idiomas (*El Hobbit*, *El Señor de los Anillos*, *El granjero Egidio de Ham*, *El herrero de Wooton Mayor* y *El Silmarillion*), y cómo sólo un puñado de idiomas incluía más de una docena de obras traducidas (sueco, holandés, alemán, italiano y español).

Durante mi visita al archivo Tolkien de la Universidad de Marquette en 2011, tuve oportunidad de consultar la Colección Especial de la Biblioteca Raynor Memorial. En aquel momento, las obras de Tolkien se habían traducido a unos 50 idiomas. La más antigua se remonta a 1947 con la traducción sueca de *El Hobbit*; muchas traducciones , principalmente de *El Hobbit* y *El Señor de los Anillos*, se llevaron a cabo durante las décadas de 1960 y 70. Glen GoodKnight menciona el Index Translationum, publicado por la UNESCO, como una de las fuentes que utilizó en su investigación, aunque consideró que no era completamente confiable ni completa. Aunque estoy de acuerdo con GoodKnight, creo que es un punto de partida inestimable al momento de llevar a cabo una investigación en relación con las diferentes traducciones de determinado texto. Desgraciadamente, debido a la pandemia, la UNESCO y todas las oficinas relacionadas se están centrando naturalmente en

Table of First Date of Publication

	English	Swedish	Dutch	German	Polish	Portuguese	Spanish	Japanese	Italian	Afrikaans	Danish	Hebrew	French	Norwegian	Czech	Finnish	Slovak	Bulgarian	Hungarian	Rumanian	Serbo-Croat	Russian	Estonian	Indonesian	Greek	Icelandic	Catalan	Armenian	Ukrainian	Moldavian	Faeroese	Esperanto	Latvian
Hobbit	37	47	60	57	60	62	64	65	73		69	76	69	72	73	73	73	75	75	75	75	76	77	78	78	78	83	84	85	87	90	91	91
LotR	54	59	56	69	61	74	77	72	67		68	79	72	73	90	73			90	81		81	82			88	86						
Giles	49	61	71	70	62	86	81	75	75		89	68	74	80	90	78		88				86	86		80		79	88					
Tom	62	72	74	84		86		75	80		89	84	75																				
Smith	67	72	68	79	80	86	81	75	76	68	85	83	74		90	83			84	87							88						
Tree	64	72	77	82				76			87	92	74									91											
Niggle	45		71	79		86	81	75								90									80								
Fairy	45							84			73																						
Beo	37	75						84																									
E&W	63	75																															
Home	53	80									76																						
Silma	77	79	78	79	85	84	84	82	78		78	90	78		79												◇						
Father	76	76	76	78				82	76		80		77																				
Pref	40	75																															
Tales	80	82	81	83		85	88		81				88			86																	
Letters	81		83	91									90																				
Appx		80	80	81					87																								
Bliss	83		83	83					87		84		83	◇																			
Vice	84		84																														
LT1	84	◇		86				90	86																								
LT2	84	◇		87				90	87																								
Pict									89																								
Bilbo	90		91																														

underlined = printed together wih other titles

◇ = the book exists but publication date is either not known or verfied

italic = year of publication in doubt

(GoodKnight 1992, 62)

asuntos más urgentes y el sitio se encuentra en estos momentos fuera de servicio. Sería importante que alguna persona dedicada a estudiar la obra de Tolkien mantuviera una base de datos actualizada que dé cuenta de todas las traducciones disponibles de sus obras en diferentes idiomas y variantes dialectales, así como de toda la información relevante sobre los traductores y las editoriales, tal y como hizo GoodKnight en su momento.

La primera traducción de *El Hobbit* al español no fue la edición de 1982 realizada por Manuel Figueroa para Minotauro que todo el mundo conoce en los países hispanohablantes, sino *El Hobito* (1964) de la traductora argentina Teresa Sánchez Cuevas. El investigador de la traducción Jorge Fondebrider, retomando una célebre máxima, señala que los clásicos deben ser retraducidos cada diez o quince años.[2] Existe, por tanto, un espacio para una muy necesaria nueva traducción al español, ya sea al castellano o, preferiblemente, a una de las muchas variantes dialectales latinoamericanas, ya que la diferencia semántica entre esas variantes es a menudo mayor que la que existe entre variantes de otras lenguas, sobre todo si tenemos en cuenta cómo se representa la oralidad en las obras literarias que incluyen un componente híbrido. El profesor Mark Hooker explica que los traductores que se embarcan en la producción de versiones de las obras de Tolkien "deberían ser conscientes de la naturaleza híbrida del texto de Tolkien e intentar reproducirla" (Hooker 2004).[3]

Otro aspecto del mismo conflicto es que muchas obras *de* Tolkien, incluidas publicaciones muy recientes, se han traducido

2. "La lengua cambia y, como la lengua cambia, cambian las modas de traducción [...] se supone que cada diez o quince años los clásicos deben ser retraducidos" ("Corazón de tinieblas", 2021)
3. "Los traductores que emprendan la 'traducción' de Tolkien deben ser conscientes de la naturaleza híbrida del texto de Tolkien e intentar reproducirla. 'Los textos híbridos permiten la introducción en una cultura meta de conceptos hasta ahora desconocidos y/o socialmente inaceptables/ no aceptados a través de un medio que, por su no conformidad con las convenciones y normas sociales/estilísticas, proclama la alteridad de su origen y legitima así su derecho a ser escuchado. Hay una libertad de expresión que no se ve obstaculizada por dichas convenciones', afirman Schäffner y Adab en su obra 'The Concept of the Hybrid Text in Translation.' Los traductores que ignoran la naturaleza híbrida del texto de Tolkien están rechazando la reivindicación legítima de que se perciba la otredad de su texto". (Hooker, 2004, traducción propia).

a muchas de las lenguas mayoritarias europeas y asiáticas, pero desgraciadamente no ocurre lo mismo con la mayoría de las obras *sobre* Tolkien, y eso plantea un problema en dos vertientes: la investigación escrita en inglés no está llegando a muchos estudiosos que sólo son hablantes de otras lenguas y, lo que es probablemente más grave, casi ninguna investigación de las realizadas por estudiosos que son hablantes nativos de otras lenguas está llegando al público angloparlante si no se publica en inglés, en ambos casos debido a la falta de traducciones. Esto es evidente en español donde una de las pocas obras que han sido traducidas son los volúmenes de John Garth, *Tolkien y la Gran Guerra* y *Los mundos de JRR Tolkien*, ambos publicados por Minotauro y traducidos por el Dr. Martin Simonson y el Dr. Eduardo Segura. Ambos traductores tienen una bien ganada reputación como académicos, y ambos han participado también en el proyecto de traducción de obras de Tolkien como *Beren y Luthien* y *La historia de Kullervo*, también publicadas por Minotauro.[4] Sin pretender desacreditar la erudición de Garth, es evidente que la relación que existe entre los traductores y la editorial, así como la sólida reputación académica de los investigadores, podrían explicar, al menos en parte, por qué estas obras se han traducido al español mientras que docenas de otras obras fundamentales en los Estudios sobre Tolkien aún no lo han sido.

---

4. Esta editorial ha publicado la traducción al español de la famosa biografía de Tolkien escrita por Humphrey Carpenter; *El arte de El Señor de los Anillos* y *El arte de El Hobbit* de Wayne Hammond; los dos volúmenes de Catherine Mcilwaine relacionados con la exposición *Tolkien Maker of Middle-Earth* de 2018 en la Bodleian Library; *LOTR Sketchbook* de Alan Lee; *A Middle-Earth Traveler: Sketches from Bag End to Mordor*, de John Howe; cuatro libros de David Day, así como un par de libros de cocina y libros para colorear. Todas estas obras son traducciones de textos escritos originalmente en inglés; lamentablemente, no es de extrañar que aún no haya libros en su catálogo sobre Tolkien traducidos de otros idiomas.

A la hora de considerar de qué manera se han traducido los textos sobre Tolkien escritos en lengua española, un claro ejemplo es *El Tío Curro* de José Manuel Ferrández Bru (2018), quien ha examinado la conexión de Tolkien con España a través del padre Francis Morgan. La recepción académica de *Uncle Curro* ha sido muy positiva; sin duda una hazaña bien merecida, que se ha debido en parte a las buenas críticas, entre ellas la de John Garth (que escribió el prefacio para la edición inglesa), a su disponibilidad en inglés y a la presencia de su autor en los círculos académicos en lengua inglesa a través de publicaciones en espacios como *Mallorn* y *Tolkien Studies* (2018).[5] Además, al consultar a la doctora Holly Ordway, autora de *Tolkien's Modern Reading* (2021), si había identificado a algún escritor en lengua española del que pudiera afirmar que había sido leído por Tolkien, me remitió a Ferrández Bru para más información. Esto demuestra cómo su obra ha permeado en los estudios sobre Tolkien en lengua inglesa gracias a la presencia de la traducción al inglés.[6]

Si esto ocurre con los trabajos académicos, ¿nos podemos imaginar qué sucede con las contribuciones de los fans de todo el mundo en tantos idiomas diferentes, muchas de ellas dignas

---

5. Entre otras investigaciones de Ferrández Bru pueden mencionarse "Wingless fluttering: Some Personal Connections in Tolkien's Formative Years" en *Tolkien Studies: An Annual Scholarly Review*, Vol. 8.; "J. R. R. Tolkien's 'second father' Fr. Francis Morgan and other non-canonical influences", en *The Return of the Ring*, Luna Press Publishing, 2012; y "J. R. R. Tolkien and the Spanish Civil War", en *Mallorn*, no. 51, mayo de 2011, pp. 16-19, https://journals.tolkiensociety.org/mallorn/article/view/78.

6. No es el caso, por desgracia, de muchos estudiosos hispanohablantes, así como de otras lenguas, que hasta hace muy poco apenas han estado representados, y eso sobre todo gracias a congresos y seminarios como los organizados por la Tolkien Society o la Mythopoetic Society. Es el caso, por ejemplo, del artículo de Pedro Angeles-Ruiz publicado en las actas de la Tolkien Society de 2005, el volumen *The Ring Goes Ever On* (agradezco a la Dra. Laura Michel que me lo haya señalado).

de reconocimiento, ya sea por su calidad o por su impacto? Lawrence Venuti ha afirmado en repetidas ocasiones que para gran parte de los lectores a escala mundial el único material disponible es el que se produce en inglés o se traduce a esta lengua (Venuti 1992, 5-6 *passim*). Por desgracia es natural que el trabajo de los fans rara vez llegue a traducirse si no es gracias a proyectos de colaboración de traductores no profesionales con quienes el público está en deuda (Evans 2019, 179; McDonough Dolmaya 2019, 127). En su obra *Translation, Rewriting and the Manipulation of Literary Fame*, André Lefevere se ha referido a las razones por las que algunas obras pueden llegar a un público más amplio gracias a la traducción, identificando algunos de los factores que influyen en las decisiones sobre cuáles obras se traducen y cuáles no (1992, 26-9 *passim*). A este respecto, Robin Reid y Michael Ellam han analizado cómo es que el legado de Tolkien es aprobado por sus lectores:

> Aunque nadie puede limitar las distintas maneras en que las obras de Tolkien se reformulan y reelaboran, nadie se atrevería a negar el impulso de juzgar dichas reformulaciones y reelaboraciones en términos de autenticidad, es decir, si mantienen la fidelidad al original. Pero entonces, ¿quién define y aprueba esa fidelidad? ¿Es posible siquiera aprobar a Tolkien? Tal vez, sin embargo, plantearse tales preguntas de por sentado un mérito artístico similar al de otras obras en lengua inglesa que sirven repetidamente como fuentes para la adaptación (*Beowulf, Los cuentos de Canterbury*, los dramas de Shakespeare, etc.). El hecho de que las obras de Tolkien sean adaptadas de forma tan amplia y variada por tantas personas, y en muchos casos de forma muy apasionada, da testimonio de su importancia intrínseca, hasta el punto de que no hay que alarmarse por aquellas adaptaciones que parecieran alejarse mucho de lo que las fuentes parecen contener o desarrollar (Reid & Elam 2016, 2).

La cantidad de críticas que se desprenden de cualquier obra de arte, así como las diferentes obras de creación inspiradas en ella, son prueba de su relevancia en una determinada etapa de la historia; en este caso, también de su valor artístico. La multicitada frase de Tolkien tomada de su carta a Milton Wadman (identificada con el número 130 en el libro de Humphrey Carpenter) se ha utilizado como si fuese una autorización del propio Tolkien para producir otras obras que se originen en su *Legendarium*. No obstante, las grandes obras de arte no pueden predeterminar de qué manera serán recibidas por el público una vez que han salido de la pluma y de las manos del escritor, del mismo modo que las academias no pueden regular la manera en que los distintos pueblos van a adoptar, y a adaptar, una lengua. La lengua es un organismo vivo en continua evolución, y dicha evolución depende de los usuarios de la lengua, de los pueblos que la hablan y la transforman; lo mismo puede decirse de las obras maestras: la forma en que evolucionen dependerá no sólo del artista, el subcreador, quien se encuentra del lado del emisor en el modelo de comunicación, sino también del público, de los lectores, quienes están en el otro extremo, del lado del receptor.

En el texto citado, Lefevere se refiere al impacto que tienen las antologías en el momento de decidir qué obras tienen más probabilidades de sobrevivir : "El proceso que tiene como consecuencia la aceptación o el rechazo, la canonización o no canonización de las obras literarias está dominado [...] por factores muy concretos [...] como el poder, la ideología, la institución y la manipulación [...] [L]a escritura en todas sus formas ocupa una posición predominante entre [tales] factores concretos" (1992, 2). Cuando Reid y Ellam analizan la evolución de las obras seleccionadas por Zimbardo e Isaacs en sus diferentes antologías, se refieren al "reconocimiento comúnmente aceptado de *El Señor de los Anillos* como obra maestra, un objetivo que se alcanzó no [sólo] por los méritos de la obra en sí, sino ...en parte debido a los más de cincuenta años de investigación académica, razón por la cual es importante señalar la necesidad de ampliar los estudios sobre Tolkien para incluir trabajos sobre las adaptaciones, así como aquellos que son llevados a cabo por estudiosos que han recibido su formación en una variedad más amplia de disciplinas" (2016, 6).

Durante el Seminario de Verano organizado por la Tolkien Society, varias ponencias se centraron en la necesidad de una mayor presencia de varios grupos minoritarios subrepresentados, entre ellos, los hablantes de lenguas distintas al inglés. La labor que realizan instituciones públicas, editoriales y asociaciones para ofrecer una mayor visibilidad a estos colectivos es de suma importancia; de ahí la relevancia del Seminario de este año. La existencia de una lengua implica la existencia de un conjunto único de conceptos y de una visión del mundo totalmente distinta. Como en el caso de *El Principito*, los valores de la obra de Tolkien, tanto éticos como estéticos, artísticos y de aplicación a la vida cotidiana, darán un fruto diferente en los hablantes de hña hñu en México, que en los hablantes de inuktitut, la lengua de los inuit, y su apreciación y análisis habrán de enriquecer el suelo donde sean trasplantados.

How Queer Atheists, Agnostics, and Animists Engage with Tolkien's Legendarium[1]

Robin Anne Reid

This project was inspired in part by Verlyn Flieger's article, "But What Did He Really Mean?," in which she argues that J.R.R. Tolkien's multiple contradictory statements in his fiction, non-fiction, and letters create the opportunity for conflicting readings about Tolkien and religion to flourish.[2] As a result, both Christian and neo-pagan fans claim the work, and the author, as an advocate for their beliefs. Flieger concludes that *The Lord of the Rings* is "a book from which readers have been taking what they want and need for sixty years and show no signs of stopping" (162). My immediate response to Flieger's essay, especially given the rise in religious-political conflicts occurring in the United States and other nations during the 21st century, which are affecting online fandom discursive spaces, was to wonder about how readers, such as myself, who are ignored or criticized in Tolkien discursive spaces, have been reading and taking what we want from Tolkien's work for decades (5.5 decades in my case!). I was a lukewarm Presbyterian as a child who became a Wiccan in my twenties and then an atheist in my

1. I'd like to thank Will Sherwood for all the work he and the Tolkien Society did not only to schedule the first Society event on diversity but to deal with those who opposed and wished to cancel any discussion of topics relating to alterity, diversity, identities and political ideas that have been marginalized or suppressed in the past.
2. Flieger, Verlyn. "But What Did He Really Mean?" *Tolkien Studies*, vol. 11, 2014, pp. 149-166.

fifties although I have believed in an animist universe since I first read *The Lord of the Rings* when I was ten.

I developed a research project to extend Flieger's argument through a reception approach in which I asked actual readers how they engaged with Tolkien's legendarium, focusing on atheists, agnostics, animists, and other participants in New Age movements. What these different terms mean is complicated and contradictory, as my data shows, but my goal was to include anyone who does not accept the concept of an omnipotent deity who created and reigns over the universe whatever their spirituality or belief system. The only scholarly work in Tolkien studies I have found that acknowledges atheism is Stephen Morillo's essay, 'The Entwives: Investigating the Spiritual Core of *The Lord of the Rings*.'[3] Morillo identifies himself as a "life-long atheist," and he questions the ubiquitous characterizing of Tolkien's work as "Christian," arguing that "Tolkien's own imagination produced a spiritual sensibility" that "[combined] the Norse paganism that he studies and [his imagined] peculiar medievalism" (106).

I developed an online survey for my project that was reviewed by my university's, Texas A&M-Commerce's, Institutional Review Board (IRB). The survey used a mixed methodology approach, meaning I gathered quantitative (numerical) and qualitative (written responses) data. I collected some demographic information but no personal or identifying information and asked participants to respond to eight open-ended questions. The demographic categories and questions are provided in the Appendix, "Section I: Survey Information." Respondents could answer all the survey questions in their

---

3. Morillo, Stephen. "The Entwives: Investigating the Spiritual Core of *The Lord of the Rings*." *The Ring and the Cross: Christianity and The Lord of the Rings*, ed. Paul Kerry, Fairleigh Dickinson UP, 2011, pp. 106-18.

own words rather than selecting from a pre-determined list or scale; they could also choose not to answer one or more of the questions and still complete the survey. I sent the link to my survey to online groups interested in Tolkien and collected 113 completed surveys between December 1, 2018 and January 31, 2019. I discarded one survey because it was from a theist whose responses showed a clear opposition to the purpose of my project. I have given several presentations discussing different sets of the respondents and will be working on a book that will try to show the richness and depth of the responses. Given the present limitations, I've chosen to describe the demographics of this group of respondents and then move to analysis of selected open-ended question.

This paper focuses on the respondents who identified themselves as asexual, bisexual, gay, lesbian, pansexual, queer, or some combination.[4] Table 1 shows the analysis of the 38 surveys into broad categories, with some specific sub-categories using the terminology provided by respondents. The largest percentage of respondents, 70%, are bisexual and/or pansexual, while 13% are asexual and another 13% are queer. The smallest categories were gay (2%) and lesbian (2%).[5]

---

4. The programme announcement for the Seminar resulted in a backlash among alt-right critics, especially against the presentations using queer or transgender theories, that I covered in my Dreamwidth journal and which is the focus of an essay I'm writing on the attacks on "Tolkien and Diversity," covering not only the attacks on participants in this event but on the trailers for the Amazon Prime adaptation ("Response to Backlash Against Tolkien and Diversity Seminar, *Tolkien_on_the_Web*, July 2, 2020, https://tolkien-on-the-web.dreamwidth.org/4231.html).

5. I set aside surveys from respondents who identified as het, straight, or heterosexual, as well as three who identified their sexual orientation as "cis"; one who replied to the question with "Sorry, this does not compute" [this respondent gave the same answer for most of the demographic questions]; two who chose not to reply; and another five whose responses I thought

Table 1: Sexual Orientation

BROAD CATEGORY	SUB-CATEGORY (Individual terms)	NUMBER	PERCENTAGE
Asexual	Asexual 3	5	13%
	Gray Ace, biromantic		
	None (asexual in practice)		
Bisexual/ Pansexual	Bisexual 21	27	70%
	Bisexual/Pansexual 3		
	Demisexual, bisexual 1		
	Pansexual 1		
	Pansexual/ Bisexual 1		
Gay		1	2%
Lesbian		1	2%
Queer	Queer 4	5	13%
	Queer (bi/pan) 1		
TOTAL		**38**	**100%**

After reviewing this data, I realized that the best umbrella term for the group was Alexander Doty's second definition of "queer," which is one of six that he argues show the various meanings of the word as it is used in queer theory and scholarship. This definition functions as an "umbrella term:

emphasized normativity if not straightness. These five responses were "mostly straight" (2); "straight-ish" (1); "prefer het have done homo" (1); and "heterosexual to asexual" (1). The resulting 38 surveys, which were 34% of the total 112 responses, show that people in gender, romantic, and sexual minorities are more represented among Tolkien fans than among the general population.

a. to pull together lesbian, and/or gay, and/or bisexual with little or no attention to differences (similar to certain uses of "gay" to mean lesbians, gay men, and sometimes, bisexuals, transsexuals, and transgendered people)" (2000, 6-7).

The majority of the 38 respondents, 61%, identify as Female/Cis Female/Woman; Male respondents (none of whom provided any modifiers) make up 18%. Agender people are 8% and non-binary 10%. One respondent answered but provided no specific term.[6]

Table 2: Gender

BROAD CATEGORY	SUB-CATEGORY (Individual terms)	NUMBER	PERCENTAGE
Agender	Agender	3	8%
	Agender (afab)		
	None, gender-neutral		
Female/ Woman	Female 20	23	61%
	Cis Female 2		
	Woman 1		
Male		7	18%
Non-Binary		4	10%
Shrugs	*shrug emoji* Your guess is as good as mine	1	3%
TOTAL		38	100%

Table 3 shows the ages of the 38 respondents ranged from 18-64, with the majority (61%) between 21-37 years old.

---

6. This respondent answered most of the demographic questions with, "Sorry, this does not compute."

Table 3: Age

AGE	NUMBER	PERCENTAGE
18-19	4	10%
21-29	12	32%
30-37	11	29%
41-49	7	18%
51-57	2	5%
63-64	2	5%
TOTAL	**38**	**100%**

Table 4 shows the age they remember first reading something by Tolkien. Half were 8-12 years old, all reading on their own; about a quarter were 4-7 years (some read to by parents), and the remaining quarter were in their teens, with the oldest reported first reading age being 20. While I asked only for their age, a number took advantage of the open-ended opportunity to share details about their first reading and additional readings.[7]

Table 4: Age of First Tolkien Reading

AGE	NUMBER	PERCENTAGE
4-7	9	22%
8-12	19	50%
13-20	11	28%
TOTAL	**38**	**100%**

---

7. See the Appendix, "II: Age Of First Reading Comments" for additional information they provided. Three of the nine respondents, ages 4-7, were first read Tolkien by their parents. I also realized as I was analyzing the data that I should have thought to ask what their religious affiliation or identification was when they first read Tolkien. I may do a follow-up through email which was noted as a possibility in my original IRB proposal.

My analysis of the responses to some of the open-ended questions is an ethnographic approach rather than a quantitative one. The categories that I use in the tables are driven by what the responders said rather than my pre-determined choices. My process involved reading and re-reading the responses to identify key words and phrases which I then used to group responses. The categories used in the tables below mostly come from my work with all 112 surveys although, as has been the case all along, the re-reading I did with this group added some new, more specific categories, or sub-categories. I consider the real value of this project to be the richness of the information, ideas, and interpretations from my survey respondents.

The tables in this presentation contain two categories that came out of the analysis of this group's 38 responses: "both/and," and "mixed." However, the "It's complicated /It Depends" category emerged from my very first read through of all responses. Please note that all the quotations from respondents reproduced exactly as they wrote them; I decided not to do any editing for grammar or spelling at this point.

The first open-ended question I asked all respondents was how they would describe themselves (atheist, agnostic, animist, secular, or some other term). The 38 respondents include some people who identify as atheists, some who identify as agnostics, and a group which includes animists, pagans, polytheists, one "nominal" Buddhist," one "Recovering" Catholic, one Deist as well as humanists and sceptics. Table 5 shows the different categories. A selection of comments from the survey show complex and at times contradictory definitions of the terms. especially for "atheist" and "agnostic" as well as people choosing several terms to describe their beliefs.[8]

8. A study by Moise Karim and Vassilis Saroglou, "Being Agnostic, Not Atheist: Personality, Cognitive, and Ideological Differences" confirms

Table 5: Self-Description

SELF-DESCRIPTION	NUMBER	PERCENTAGE
Atheist	14	38%
Agnostic	13	34%
Animist	5	13%
Secular	0	0
Some Other Term: Deist: 1 Pagan: 3 Affiliation: 2	5	15%
TOTAL	**38**	**100**

I wanted to know about people's experiences with organized religion. Table 6 shows that 37% identified negative experiences with a variety of denominations, institutions, and people, but that the remaining 63% had either neutral or limited experience (33%), or positive (10%), or a mix of positive and negative (10%). The last category here is one that showed up early in my analysis of the responses: "it's complicated/needs more work" (10%) and is based on the comments.[9]

the complex psychological and ideological complexity of the terms and identifications of "nonbelievers" as well as the lack of research done on the different meanings and beliefs. See the Appendix, "III. Identification As Atheist, Agnostic, Animist, Secular, Or Some Other Term Comments," for the range of meanings shared by respondents.
9. See the Appendix, "IV: Experiences with Organized Religion Comments."

Table 6: Experiences with Organized Religion

CATEGORY	NUMBER	PERCENTAGE
Negative	14	37%
Neutral or Limited	12	33%
Positive	4	10%
Positive & Negative	4	10%
It's Complicated	4	10%
TOTAL	**38**	**100%**

The above categories were fairly easy to develop, although the additional information provided by respondents complicates the question of what "atheist" and "agnostic" mean. However, the process became much more complicated with regard to political identification and nationality because what is considered "conservative" vs. "centrist" vs. "liberal" differs from country to country (and changes over time). I grouped the information for Nationality, Ethnicity, and Political Identification in Table 7 as a placeholder to allow more time for researching national political definitions in order to analyze this information.

Table 7

NATIONALITY	ETHNICITY	POLITICAL ID
American/US 22	White/Caucasian/ northern European: 20 Amerindian European 1 South Asian 1	Liberal/radical/green/ progressive 20 Libertarian 1 Somewhere between non-state socialism and anarcho-syndicalism 1

American-Canadian	East Asian/Han Chinese	No answer
Bulgarian	Bulgarian	Environmentalist, Socialist
Canadian	White descendant of Scottish settlers	Progressive
Dutch	No Answer	Democrat
France	Caucasian	Left-wing
German 2	Caucasian, White	Democrat, Social Democrat
Indian/American	Asian-Indian	Leftist
Italian	White	Democrat (very liberal)
Mexican	Lathin	Independent progressive
Russian	Russian	Democrat
Swedish 2	Caucasian, Swedish	Officially unenrolled. (In Massachusetts, they let you decide party on the day of the primary.) Generally vote with Democrats, though. Socialist/social democratic
UK	White	Leftist
Welsh	White British	Democrat by party & progressive in identification
Welsh (my passport only says British)	White Welsh	Democrat

Doty argues that none of the definitions of "queer" or related terms require the assumption of a "radical, progressive, or even liberal position on gender, sexuality or other issues," and warns against assuming the term is "reserved only for those approaches, positions, and texts that are in some way progressive" (6). As a result, I did not assume that all my respondents would identify as progressive, nor did I put any requirements for participation beyond being a legal adult who did not believe in an omnipotent god.

While the meaning of ethnic and political terminology in the responses differs depending on national context, it seems clear that this group of respondents identify themselves as left of center. Generally, 58% of the respondents are American, with the remaining 42% coming from a number of other countries. The vast majority are white. I suspect the causes are flaws in my research process, including what social media platforms I used, and Black, Indigenous, and People of Color's (BIPOC) well-founded distrust of white academics' data-gathering,

The remaining two open-ended questions elicited the most complex responses of the survey. I have provided a number of quotes that exemplify the variety of responses I received to both questions as well as the categories. Table 8 is my analysis of responses to "what makes Tolkien's work important to you?" I've identified four categories. The first is "Gender" which includes responses which focus on the structural, or literary, elements of Tolkien's work (plot, character, theme) and /or his importance to the genre of fantasy; the second, "Personal Connection" and "It Changes Over Time" include more personal information; the fourth are those responses which include two or more of the first three categories.

Table 8: What Makes Tolkien Important

CATEGORY	NUMBER	PERCENTAGE
Genre	19	53%
Personal Connection	10	28%
It Changes Over Time	3	8%
Both/and (two or more from above)	4	11%
TOTAL	**36**	**100%**

Over half the respondents emphasize genre elements, the structural and thematic literary elements, as the most important elements for them (53%). Personal connections, identified by the use of more first-person language than in the genre category, are most important for 36% of the respondents who make a direct connection between Tolkien's work and their lives. About a quarter of the respondents, 28%, explain how Tolkien helped them deal with their lives during adolescence to influencing their choices of professions as adults. A small group, 8%, emphasize that the personal connection has been life-long with the meaning of Tolkien's work changing as they read it at different times. Another 10% emphasize genre elements plus some personal connection.

Genre

I enjoy the worldbuilding, the scale of it, the mythological scope, but also the glimpses of character in the Silmarillion. It's multifaceted, and it's also impossible to ignore it's influence on my favourite genre of literature

The plot is very engaging, and the themes universal.

The overarching message of hope in the face of despair; the deep roots in Celtic and Germanic myth; the environmental overtones and reverence for the earth; the role of the artist and creator as deeply spiritual and important and heroic, and even holy (the subcreator being akin to The Creator)

I love the depth of the world he created! I also love the linguistic aspects and the repeated motifs

Their focus on friendship, sense of mythic weight, and unapologetic view of small bits of heroism

It's long meditation on the balance between ego and community reaction and actions based on the evidence of longer termed truths

The complexity of his thinking, the variety of themes explored. He's writing these fantastic adventures that are fun, imaginative, enteraining, and all that wonderful stuff of fantasy, but at the same time he's exploring deep philosophical issues from the nature of death to the ideal of leadership, from the relationship of the individual to society to the ground of ethical living.

Personal Connection

Tolkien has given my life meaning. When I was younger I had a hard time believing that Ea did not exist. In fact I was sure it existed. In some way I kind of hope that it exists in this vast universe. It is to me as Tolkien was a messenger who dedicated his life to delivering this history to us as it is far greater than anything done before.

A sense of nostalgia for my childhood.

The pattern of his characters making bad decisions and/or having bad things happen to them, and then having to live with the consequences; and the morally ambiguous characters themselves. The first strongly reminds me of real people struggling to live with their mental illnesses, specifically PTSD and depression, and the depiction of such things is very important to me, especially when it's cast in a non-judgemental light. And moral ambiguity is so rarely done well in fantasy, and even more rarely is it taken as far as it is in the Silmarillion.

They are the basis of my own spiritual beliefs, and what got me interested in being a medievalist.

They were a huge part of my teens, especially. From age 9-25 I read LotR 40 times. I am not exaggerating. I guess that trilogy was my favorite way to escape the world.

Escapism, the connection to fellow fans (my partner and my father first among them), an interest in older cultures

Change Over Time

I find something different every time I return to them. I admire the depth of his thought about his invented worlds; I rarely notice gaps, so I find his workmanship a masterclass in writing. I am also fascinated by how he used his sources.

every time i read lotr it's applicable to where i am in my life. reading it as a teenager showed me that life could have purpose and true companionship was something to be sought. now it gives me hope that darkness will pass as long as we keep working toward that goal. and the movies help a lot when i am greiving my grandfather since ian mckellen as gandalf reminds me of him.

As a teen, it was the first book that truly tied up what literary fantasy could be. As an academic, it was my first assay into pop culture – at that time. As a father, I remember reading the Hobbit to my daughter.

Both/And

The stories themselves resonate; I find that the characters and their responses to their experiences offer rich ground for analysis, empathy, and simply getting caught up in a story. I love fantasy as a genre and medieval-ish fantasy in particular. I also find that both the Silmarillion and the Lord of the Rings are useful reminders about the importance of fighting battles despite the apparent impossibility of winning, and of fighting in small and often uncredited ways; my field of work, providing civil legal assistance to indigent clients, often feels like an unwinnable cause against a much more powerful system, and Tolkien reminds me that it's nevertheless worth doing.

when i was younger it was about escape. it let me ignore my reality of depression, self harm, and suicidal thoughts. now it is one of my homes. i can see myself in the gentle hobbits but most of all i find myself in the dwarves that the word has beaten and battered down. the works are important to me because that connection, that ability to relate to the characters, to cry and mourn for their struggles or their pain has kept me alove and knowing i am not as unfeeling as the world would have me believe.

Finally, Table 9 identifies the range of responses to the question about how respondents feel or think about the common assumption that Tolkien's religion must be part of any interpretation. The categories are based on the work I've done with all the surveys, but the numbers and percentages refer only to the 38 responses. Almost a third of the group rejects, fairly comprehensively, that assumption, while 71% accept it but with increasing limitations as shown below in categories, and with longer personal responses that show more active engagement with the complexities of what it means to consider authorial intent in the context of individual readers' choices.

Table 9: Response to Assumption of Christian Meaning

RESPONSE	SUB-GROUP	PERCENTAGE
REJECTS	**10**	**26%**
Rejects assumption completely	7	
Rejects plus negative evaluation of gatekeeping readers (as narrow, shallow).	3	
ACCEPTS	**21**	**55%**
Accepts as useful or valid but not required or necessary	6	

Accepts but as no more/less important than other biographical or cultural information about author and influences (Norse myths); or no more important than other themes/meanings, or applied only to certain works (*The Silmarillion*)	5	
Accepts that it affects Tolkien's storytelling, but reader's personal worldview is important or, more strongly, readers should not be limited by author's intent ('death of author')	10	
IT DEPENDS/COMPLICATED	**7**	**19%**
More complex: has never heard of assumption, explains areas of acceptance and rejection; other specific information that differ from other categories	7	
TOTAL	**38**	**100%**

Rejects assumption completely: There are three main categories here: the 26% who reject the assumption, to varying degrees and for various reasons, the 55% who accept the assumption to some degree, with different limitations, and the 19% whose responses are more like analytical debates about the assumption. The first sub-category are those who reject the assumption.

Tolkien strongly was against metaphoric interpretations of his work. I can not deny that his strong beliefs influenced his work. However as for me fantasy is a way of escaping from this world, I absolutely refuse to read his works with a religious lense.

I reject it that assumption, and through fan fiction, I have challenged it.

It seems nonsensical to me. Mythology is crucial to human beings, but that doesn't equate to religion per se.

No, you don't, after reading his letters I think it is not necessary to share his beliefs
I learnt an expression called "bless your heart" in Texas. It completely encapsulates the snark and apathy I feel when I hear this stuff.

I don't give it much credence, and hadn't really thought it much. There are universal themes such as sacrifice for the good of all, but I don't see them as religious per se.

The second sub-category are those who reject the assumption as well as commenting on specific experiences with people they have encountered who insisted on what I'm calling the "Christian/Allegorical" reading, that the Christian meaning is the only correct meaning. The problem is not that a reader sees a Christian theme or message in the work but those readers who insist on a single "true" reading and attempt to gatekeep Tolkien's work and/or fandom communities. I have seen attempts to do so in both fandom spaces and scholarship, as have some of my respondents.

i think it's one way to look at it, but i find it short sighted to always look at tolkien's work in that way. when talking to people who insist on religious readings i generally lose respect for them

I don't find an author's own views terribly interesting except insofar as it adds depth to their writing – certainly one can look for Catholic influences and find them, but organised religion in Middle-earth seems to be non-existent, and the Valar and Eru aren't Christianity by any means. (And while I may be unfair since I don't seek out analysis through the lens of religion, much of what I have come across seems a bit shallow – you don't often see people talking about the drowning of Numenor, for example.)

I can see how this may lead to fruitful readings; I just do not think these are the only valid readings (actually, they are often uninteresting to me), both because Tolkien intended his work to be "secular" and because I do not often care about authorial intent to begin with

Accepts the assumption to some degree: Of those readers who accept some variant of the assumption, the first sub-category are readers who accept the assumption that Tolkien's religion influences his work and that it could lead to useful or valid interpretations but reject that it is required or necessary for all.

I feel the beliefs of any author, be they religious or political, CAN be taken into consideration when reading their works of fiction. But they don't HAVE TO figure into any reader's personal interpretation of the work.

I think it helps explain why Tolkien made certain narrative choices. So I would say that the knowledge enriches the text but I don't consider it necessary to enjoy his works. That said, when this leads to circular debates where everyone is repeating their side and nothing new is brought to the table, I dislike it.

i think you should remember it but it isn't a be all, end all. when i first read the hobbit, i had no knowledge of anything about the writer. in some ways i think that it isn't as important when you read because it's the story that is important but it is good to learn more about him after so you can be more aware of underlying themes and keep yourself from any unintentional harm you might cause others (the dwarves being caricatures for the Jewish people for example)

the same way i feel about any argument that says i must take the author's beliefs into account: that's one approach, but certainly not the only/required one.

I don't think that it is obligatory to take his beliefs into account when interpreting his work. If someone wants to, they are welcome to do so, especially if it leads them to something new, but I dislike the assumption that one must consider the religious aspect of it all.

The second sub-category are those who accept that Tolkien's religious beliefs are important and might be useful but are no more or less important than other biographical information. or themes, or, in several cases, accept it only as useful for *The Silmarillion*.

I don't always agree, but I do think its interesting to know the perspective he was writing from, as well as why he made some of the edits and changes he did.

It's obvious that the Catholicism of Tolkien influenced his work, but I don't like the idea that everything he wrote can only be interpreted in a Christian way – especially not when it's just as obvious that, say, Norse mythology had a great influence as well.

I accept this reading, particularly in relation with the Silmarillion. It sheds light on his inspirations for the theology/ cosmology of Arda and his treatment of his characters, especially male vs female characters.

I haven't really encountered it much. I don't particularly care, and don't see anything like that in his works, except in Silmarillion, with the creation story.

I'm a new historicist by inclination; I think understanding his personal beliefs and his aims a profitable way to look at Tolkien's work, though by no means the only one. There should also be a place for interpreting it WITHOUT taking into account any of his beliefs, religious or otherwise.

The third sub-category are people who argue some variant on the concept of the "death of the author," often quoting the phrase in their response. They accept that Tolkien's religion affected his story but emphasize the importance of the reader's personal worldview (whether their own, or readers in general) in interpreting the story. The emphasis on readers' worldviews and agency sets this category apart from the others although they allow that such Christian interpretations are valid for some readers.

Pfft, is my brief reaction to that. I am not a fan of prescriptivist critics. (Which is not quite the right word, but close enough.) My longer reaction is, I do think that his beliefs and religion are *one aspect* of things that *can* be taken into account when reading his work, as are things like how World War I affected him. However, it's also *possible* to read his work without letting outside influences pervade your thinking. So basically: I'm inclined to be *interested in* how many aspects of Tolkien's life influenced his writing, I just decline to be told that it's how I *must* interact with his work at all times.

I'm more of a Death of the Author type, so I'm not a huge fan of that assumption.

Tolkien's religion did play an influencing part in his works, but that is not the end-all, be-all. The works can be read without taking Tolkien's religion into account, or read eith it taken into account.

I think there is a difference between taking something into account and considering it the end-all of interpretations; there is, I believe, certain moral assumptions that come from his religious beliefs, but that does not mean that I, as a reader and fan, need to agree with them; my reading, informed by my beliefs, is valid even if it goes against the authors moral and religious stances

I don't really think so. It may help understand some of his ideas, of course, but a person can enjoy and interpret his books without this knowledge (I strongly belive in the death of the author)

I view religion or lack there of much like a person's political beliefs. They can add understanding to how/why the work was created, but the act of reading brings much of the reader to the work. An atheist reading is different than a Catholic reading of the same work.

Tolkien's religious beliefs influenced his worldbuilding heavily and there are many aspects of his works that have an overall religious feel to it. However, death of the author, his works only mean what I make of them to me. His religion is important to contextualize some motifs and "rules" within his works, but the latter transcedes the first. His perspective and storytelling lense is shaped by it, but my reading is shaped by my own worldview as well.

As "the author is dead," you certainly don't have to take his beliefs into account when viewing the texts in isolation, but if you're considering his creative process and motivations then it would seem silly not to do so.

I do believe that Tolkien's religious vantage point does shape some of the larger scale concerns in the text (the play of a fate that no one on the ground can know, ala Tom Shippey). Still there's tremendous value I find in it as a Pagan.

It Depends/It's Complicated: The third main category has the smallest percentage of responses in all of the analyses I've done, but the responses are usually longer responses as well as being more dialogic, that is, considering various positions and possible evidence for them. When I work on the longer project, I expect the responses in this category to be analyzed for a number of different sub-categories, such as those who said that they never saw religion in Tolkien's work, or learned about his religion late in life, or had never heard of this assumption from other Tolkien readers they knew. Others, however, reflect the respondents' own thinking, including citing specific evidence from Tolkien's work, contrasting his work to Lewis' more allegorical fantasy, or describing specific experiences interacting with Tolkien readers who have different ideas about the assumption.

It is possible that some of Tolkien's religious beliefs influenced his work, but at the same time, his work does not come across as overtly religious to me. There is no clear parallel for me when I ready Tolkien's works as there is when I read say the Narnia books

I agree, but I don't think his religious beliefs are inherently incompatible with a more animistic or polytheistic worldview, and I don't think his creations themselves point to the view that there is only one Truth, and that is that of the Christian God's message. I think some can read it too narrowly when they focus on his very obviously deeply held beliefs.

Eh. I kinda throw it out the window. I can see some of it in his LACE works, which makes them less palatable. I'm kinda half and half between the "death of the author" and "respect the author" camps. Tolkien himself said his works on middle earth we're not religious or historical allegory, so I'm going to take that at face value. I think if we wanted to do a very detailed close read of the text, we can see which assertions he makes that are based in Catholicism. But I don't think they make such a huge different that we would fail to appreciate the work completely if we didn't have that knowledge base. Additionally, he doesn't really use religion as a moral theme – I'd say friendship and bravery are more important there. When I see people say we need to consider his religious background, I ask why. I see it a lot in the context of analyzing privilege or cultural assumptions, which I agree with, to an extent. Like, how do his opinions on religion and politics and imperialism sneak into the text [...] that said, I don't need to pick and old manuscript published decades ago completely apart the way I would a new publication because a) the sins are small and b) we need historical context. Also, I have the historical and cultural knowledge to understand imbalances of power and injustice so I can accept how that shows up in literature and learn from it and still be able to enjoy the piece. I think purity culture is kinda toxic.

The kinds of issues Tolkien explored in his works, from morality to leadership to courage to the relationship of nature and human invention, are things that transcend any religion. All religions attempt to address some or all of these, and find various answers, they are not the property of one faith, or indeed of any faith, as it is not necessary to assume any kind of metaphysical life to conront the big questions – and the little ones. Tolkien uses the existance of supernatural beings to explore some of these idesa, but the gods are pretty much manifestations of the forces of the physical universe, and the ultimate divinity is actually vague enough that I can even read my own beliefs there if I want to. I don't think Tolkien was writing a Roman Catholic, or even a Christian mythos. He was writing a mythos in which there are things greater and vaster than mere human minds, but which every human must face, understand, and make choices about. Where do you see nature, or invention, or chaos, fitting into the shape of existence. How do you respond to the potential we have, by our conscious habitation of the physical, to give, or take, nurture or destroy, celebrate or desecrate, place the self alone above others, or integrate the self into comunity? What are the important things in life? How does one become an ethical human being?

My answer to this question has two parts. One, whether the author's beliefs must be taken into account in reading and interpreting. Two, how I as an atheist personally interact with the fact that Tolkien's work was written by someone of Tolkien's religious beliefs. I found the question very interesting. Since you say the assumption is widespread, it must be, but I can't remember encountering it. Probably because I agree with it to the point where it's invisible to me.

If the focus of a reader or critic is to interrogate the relationship between a piece of writing and the author's mind, motivating impulses, or influences, then I think that reader or critic probably does need to consider what if any influence Tolkien's religious beliefs had on his work. I also think that any critic claiming that Tolkien's work is in some way universal, either in its appeal or in its applicability, ought to qualify that claim with an acknowledgement that Tolkien's background and identity (not just religious, but racial, national, gendered, and class-based) differs from many of his readers'. But in terms of how readers approach the work, or its effect on a particular reader, or an in-universe analysis of characters and writerly moves, I think consideration of Tolkien's religious beliefs is less necessary. So I don't take issue with readers and critics who focus on Tolkien's Catholicism in their discussions of his work; only with those who assume his readers – and theirs – share certain tenets of that belief system.

77

My conclusion at this point is that: the stories people tell about reading Tolkien's work are powerful ones. I believe my project, featuring the voices and stories of Tolkien readers who are approaching the legendarium with beliefs and experiences that have not been considered in previous academic scholarship and have been marginalized or suppressed in some fandom spaces (offline as well as online) has the potential to show how much is shared by readers across the spectrum of religious and non-religious beliefs. That possibility of finding common ground is one reason why I would like to see a larger project that would focus on how readers of all faiths and those with no faith engage with Tolkien. I retired in 2020 but would welcome the chance to work with other scholars to develop a survey-based project for that purpose.

Bibliography

Doty, Alexander, *Flaming Classics: Queering the Film Canon*, (New York: Routledge, 2000).

Flieger, Verlyn, "But What Did He Really Mean?" *Tolkien Studies*, 11 (2014), 149-166.

Karim, M. and V, Saroglou. 'Being Agnostic, Not Atheist: Personalitiy, Cognivitve, and Ideological Differences,' *Psychology of Religion and Spirituality*, March 21, 2022, http://dx.doi.org/10.1037/rel0000461.

Morillo, Stephen, 'The Entwives: Investigating the Spiritual Core of *The Lord of the Rings*,' in *The Ring and the Cross: Christianity and The Lord of the Rings*, ed. By Paul Kerry, (Madison: Fairleigh Dickinson UP, 2011), pp. 106-118.

Appendix

I. SURVEY INFORMATION

Demographic Information: Gender, Sexual Orientation, Age, Ethnicity, Nationality, and Political Identification.

The eight open-ended questions were:
1. How would you describe yourself: atheist, agnostic, animist, secular, or some other term?
2. How would you describe your religious and/or spiritual beliefs if any?
3. How would you describe your experiences with organized religion?
4. How old were you when you first read something by Tolkien?
5. What are your favorite, or favorites, of Tolkien work(s)?
6. What makes Tolkien's works important to you?
7. A widespread assumption is that Tolkien's religious beliefs must be taken into account in reading and interpreting his work. How do you feel about this assumption among readers and critics when you encounter it?
8. Is there anything else about your experiences with Tolkien's work that you would like to discuss? If so, please elaborate here.
NOTE: Responses quoted below are copied/pasted exactly as written. I have not done any editing. These are representative examples, not the complete set of comments for any response.

II. AGE OF FIRST READING COMMENTS FOR TABLE 4

i believe i was at least 13 but it could have been later or even earlier.

My mother read The Hobbit to me when I was aprox. 5, I read it on my own around age 10.

Um. Does being read to by my parents count? Because if so, six. If not, probably about nine?

7? Maybe? The Hobbit was one of the first books I was read as a child, so I might have been even younger.

My mother read The Hobbit AND The Lord of the Rings to me as a child, around 7 or 8 maybe. They were the first actual novels (as opposed to things like Dr. Seuss, etc) that I read on my own, I think probably around 10 or 12.

About eight or nine – i was an early and advanced reader, loved fantasy, and the books had just been published in North America. I read LOTR first, then The Hobbit, then others as it became available to me.

I read The Hobbit shortly before my 10th birthday, and LOTR right around my 10th birthday. I asked for and got Unfinished Tales as a present for my 11th birthday and immediately finished reading what I hadn't already read standing up in the bookstore, and I'm 90% sure I read the Silmarillion before UT, so I must have read (I didn't say "understood") the Silmarillion when I was 15

My first contact with Tolkien was between age 2-6, my father used to read the Hobbit to my brother and me when we were younger. I read it myself when I was about 10.

III. IDENTIFICATION AS ATHEIST, AGNOSTIC, ANIMIST, SECULAR, OR SOME OTHER TERM COMMENTS FOR TABLE 5

Atheist

Nonexistent; I am not religious nor have any spiritual beliefs

I have none. I don't like the idea of paradise as I wish for everything to end after death. However if there is such a thing I would wish to spend the afterlife in Arda and Valinor.

I don't believe in any gods, but I do consider myself spiritual in the sense of revering the natural world and it's processes. As a scientist I am totally fascinated by the world and how it works.

I believe there is an energy to the universe, and that energy creates, inhabits, or contributes to everything in creation. I believe what we refer to as "life" is nothing more than a complex manifestation of that energy. But I don't believe in a single, sentient consciousness that controls or creates the universe.

I guess there might be something, but it seems very unlikely to me.

I was raised Hindu and still engage in some of those cultural/community practices, but am an atheist in terms of beliefs. I prefer a ethical framework that does not depend on extrinsic imposition of morality or on the promise of future reward and punishment.

De facto atheist per Richard Dawkin's scaling

Agnostic

I believe in God's existance, though I don't belive it it possible to prove it, besides, I belive that God doen't intefere in this world anymore

i think there's far more to the universe than we currently understand. and i'm fine with that.

I can't help but believe in some sort of energy in the universe but I don't think it's intelligent or morally inclined in an way

there is more to life than what we can explain, but whether or not to call that mysticism or lack of science is beyond me – I haven't really settled on any solid view

I don't believe that a higher power (specifically as depicted in Christianity) exists and I think that claiming that nothing like it can exist at all is not an argument that can be made. This is due to the fact that we as humans don't have sufficient understanding of the universe to make definitive conclusions on the subject. Therefore, it is up to each individual person to decide what they want to believe.

all the religions could be right at the same time and coexist peacefully if evangicalism was lessened or stopped completely and now i am leaning toward a more polytheistic belief almost bordering on paganism but not yet decided.

Animist

Wiccan-influenced pagan with some Christian leanings. (I'm a Unitarian Universalist, that's absolutely reasonable amongst my people.)

Mainly animist, with polytheistic leanings.

Unitarian Universalist & somewhat nebulous.

deeply nature-based; animistic and polytheistic

Some Other Term

I'm part of the Unitarian Universalist church, but do not feel I (currently) believe in a Creator

I think all religions have useful elements for understanding ourselves and how to live, but none has a monopoly on ultimate truth; Christianity and Buddhism in particular appeal to me personally. My religious practice involves learning and trying to understand what I learn.

Pagan, Paganism

Pagan witch Earth- and spirit-based

pagan/secular animist/spiritual?

Recovering Catholic I grew up Catholic, but presently, all I know is that it's impossible to know, and therefore not really worth worshipping anything.

IV. EXPERIENCES WITH ORGANIZED RELIGION COMMENTS FOR TABLE 6

Negative

Very poor.

A bittersweet sadness that it isn't something meaningful for me like it is for other members of my family

I'm from Russia, and I really despise our official religion and the Church with its hypicricy, self-righteousness and greediness

my family attended many different christian churches when i was young, before settling on LDS (Mormon). upon turning 18, i turned my back on the Mormon church and christianity due to their treatment of women and minorities.

Negative, I grew up Catholic and took it very seriously. As such it probably made my life much more difficult and continues to causse mental difficulties.

Unpleasant. I have a very, very few friends who identify as Christian and are genuinely among the nicest people I've ever known. But I live in the American south and organized religion here is a monster.

My paternal grandmother demanded I be baptized catholic. The religion never really took because a) I really disagree with the repression and inhibition of that Catholic Church b) I'm gay and they don't want me around and c) when my mom filed for divorce, they basically kicked her and me out but let my father stay, so I think they're hypocritical.

In general: not great. I dislike hierarchy & essentialism and encountered this both in the catholic church of my childhood and the New Age movements I explored during adolescence.

Neutral /Limited

Neutral; I have visited church on a few occasions, mostly with school, and felt alienated and bored. I have never had any interest in religion, either philosophical or ritual.

My grandparents are Christian and we celebrate christian holidays; my aunt and uncle are church (protestant) representatives; I have worked with humanitarian organizations sponsored by the church before

Limited

I grew up catholic, left the church when I discovered that philosophy is a thing

Very limited. I have attended services of several Christian denomination for various reasons – student at a religious school, weddings or funerals of people I've known, things like that and I've done a fair amount of reading on many religions. I've never been a member of any organised religion nor was I raised in any faith.

Around 16 tried be religious, but cannot believe in any kind of god or spiritual beings no matter how much I might have wanted to.

Positive

Generally positive; I received much support from an Anglican vicar when my grandfather died; I feel supported and part of something greater when I (rarely) attend Mass.

Generally positive within the religion of my youth

I spent years in church choirs (Protestant). I've been part of many many services, but avoided Communion since I was a teenager. I feel friendly toward that community, but I don't believe.

I attended Hindu temples somewhat frequently as a child and participated in weekly religious education classes. As an adult I have occasionally accompanied friends to organized religious gatherings in various traditions (mostly Christian and Jewish), especially where organized religious communities intersect with progressive politics and advocacy.

Positive And Negative

I hang out in both an organized religion (the UU church) and a disorganized one (the wider neo-pagan movement). These have been fulfilling and interesting experiences. I am wary of and have had less than positive experiences with some sects of Christianity.

Some okay, some really bad. I do not participate in organized religion

Good personal history with the UUs, sad dalliance with the Fundamentalists, bad family history with RCC and Baptists

when i was younger, i was raised in a nazarene Christian church. for a time my experiences were positive but as i grew, i began to doubt because the struggles i was facing were decimating my will to live. the reactions i recieved to my sexuality along with the reactions i recieved for my struggle to keep having faith, were lack luster at best and judgemental at worst. i came to the conclusion that i wasn't wanted there and why should i stick around or keep believing when all i got from it was pain and hatred.

It's Complicated

Baptized Greek Orthodox, father an American Baptist minister, mother with a degree in Religious Education who ran religious education for a while at an Episcopalian church. Was taken intermittently to all three churches as a child and discussion of religion was always a part of my life. Though I'm not a believer I find it very interesting in a social/cultural/aesthetic sense and do go to church (Orthodox) occasionally as an adult.

I was raised Catholic, but refused confirmation. I found Neo-Paganism as a teenager and have been basically living in that stream to various degrees ever since.

I grew up Catholic, but was never really sure I believed in God. I loved the ritual of the Mass, though, and as a teen, loved the image of Christ as a radical political figure.

Stars Less Strange:
An Analysis of Fanfiction and Representation within the Tolkien Fan Community

Dawn Walls-Thumma

Fanfiction based on Tolkien's world has existed longer and resulted in more stories than nearly any other fan community. By its very definition, fanfiction pushes at the boundaries of a fictional world, providing fruitful ground for explorations of how gender, race, and sexuality manifest in an imagined world that often fails to address them directly or adequately. Does Tolkien-based fanfiction do these things, and what factors influence an author's willingness to write about women, characters of color, or queer characters? What pushes authors even further to critically engage Tolkien's views, ideas, and potential shortcomings on issues of gender, race, and sexuality?

Fanfiction is a term remarkably difficult to define. Following formative scholarly work in fan studies, this paper considers fanfiction as any fictional work that transforms elements from an existing literary, media, or other text into a new work of fiction (Pugh 2005, 9; Jenkins 2013, 156). Furthermore, as Camille Bacon-Smith established in her 1992 book *Enterprising Women*, one of the earliest studies of fanfiction, fanfiction writers do not receive monetary compensation for their work but "write to comment upon or add to the canon of materials they already know" (45; see also Pugh 2005, 15-6 and Jenkins 2013, 160). The lack of a profit motive distinguishes fanfiction writers culturally from the producers of big-budget adaptations—Peter Jackson and company and now the Amazon showrunners are the most salient examples in this case—even if their creative processes look remarkably the same.

However, the differences between fanfiction and sanctioned adaptations differ in more ways than the financial compensation their creators receive (or do not). Since the outset of fanfiction studies, scholars have recognized that fanfiction communities have distinct cultures with some aspects held in common across most communities and others unique to a specific community (Bacon-Smith 1992, 48; De Kosnik 2016, 96). One aspect recognized as near-universal in fanfiction communities is the elevation of the experiences of women and queer characters (Bacon-Smith 1992, 52, 228; Pugh 2005, 20, 90; Jenkins 2013, 191). This element is so pervasive that, in her 2016 study of fanfiction archives, Abigail De Kosnik concluded that fanfiction archives are inherently both women's and queer spaces, even if their purpose was not in sharing homoerotic content (131). Sanctioned adaptations, such as the Jackson film trilogies, on the other hand, tend to retain and even amplify racist and sexist aspects of the legendarium and disregard queer readings altogether (Ibata 2003). A generation of fans once free to imagine Orcs however they please, for example, now assume they are dark-skinned and dreadlocked (Seah 2021). Women characters in heroic roles—some of them canonical (Éowyn), others elevated (Arwen), and others invented entirely (Tauriel)—still find their romantic interests centered in a way that they are not for characters like Aragorn (Gilchrist 2013; Tarhiliel). And queer characters remain entirely absent (Smol 2004, 967-8).

Fanfiction is different. Unbeholden to powerful economic interests that benefit from maintaining the status quo, fanfiction writers have the potential to transform texts to make room for typically marginalized voices. Fan studies scholars, overall, would assert this as a if not the primary purpose of fanfiction. For example, in a 2006 article, Abigail Derecho termed fanfiction the "literature of the subordinate" for its potential to open texts to perspectives and voices excluded by publishing and media industries that have only recently and feebly begun to stir toward realizing that a tiny minority of the world's population—cisgender, straight, white males—does not in fact hold *all* of the good stories (71). Tolkien scholar Una McCormack, speaking specifically of Tolkien-based fanfiction, made a similar assertion with her idea of reparative reading, which she defines as, "acts of transformation, reparation, and radicalization [...] establishing female presences, queer presences, and urban working class presences in a text chiefly concerned with the masculine and the heroic" (2015, 310). For anyone interested in more diverse stories, the possibilities represented by fanfiction become enormous and exciting.

Fanfiction, in other words, pushes outward upon the boundaries of the canon. In the context of fanfiction, *canon* is defined differently than in literature. Rather than a culture's foundational artistic works, in fanfiction, canon refers to the set of facts about a secondary world—in this case, Arda—that are accepted by the majority of fans as true of that world. While fanfiction communities vary in the importance they place on the canon, Tolkien fanfiction communities tend to highly value knowledge of the canon (Walls-Thumma 2019, 13-4). Because Tolkien's canon is far from straightforward, details and interpretations enshrined by fans as canon often reveal whose perspectives are privileged in the stories created by a particular community.

1 - History of Tolkien Fanfiction Fandom

Fanfiction about Tolkien's legendarium has existed since at least 1957, and in the age of online fanfiction, has become one of the largest, most prolific fandoms. Due to its prodigious size and longevity, therefore, this paper cannot represent every Tolkien fanfiction community, much less every Tolkien fanfiction writer, that has existed across the vast breadth and depth of its history. At its peak in the early 2000s, there were hundreds of Tolkien fanfiction groups, some with thousands of members and others with just a few. It is impossible to represent the values and practices of them all.

This paper utilizes two approaches to gather its data. First is that of a historian. Some of the early Tolkien fanfiction groups are still online; others have been archived by fandom historians over the years. When publicly available, these groups or their archives offer a glimpse at how discussions of race, gender, and sexuality unfolded at various points in the fandom's history. Secondly, the paper uses results from the Tolkien Fanfiction Survey, which I ran first in 2015 and again in 2020 in collaboration with Maria Alberto. Both surveys were IRB-approved and open to writers and readers of Tolkien-based fanfiction and, after collecting basic demographic data, consisted mostly of Likert-style items that assessed the participant's stance on statements concerning values, beliefs, and behaviors around Tolkien fanfiction. Participants were solicited through posts to social media and Tolkien fanfiction websites, and fans were encouraged to "signal boost" these posts to receive as diverse a pool of participants as possible. The 2015 survey had 1052 participants; in 2020, 746 people participated.

Tolkien's legendarium—at least in terms of mainstream readings to this point—reflects much of Western literature and media in either excluding these perspectives, such as the lack of women characters, or relegating members of a group to a stereotyped or caricatured role, such as an overreliance on dark-skinned villains (McCormack 2015, 309). There is a similar lack of queer and working-class characters. As McCormack discussed in her 2015 essay on reparative reading, fanfiction writers can address these shortcomings in several ways. First is to invent original characters belonging to marginalized groups to coexist alongside characters from the canon. Secondly, fanfiction writers can develop minor characters who belong to (or could belong to) a marginalized group. Resisting the tendency to assume a character is a straight, white male until described otherwise, for example, fanwriters commonly depict *The Silmarillion* characters Elemmirë (ungendered in the text) as a woman and Maedhros (described as unmarried) as queer (*Silmarillion*, 81; *Peoples*, 318). Finally, fanfiction writers can take a character who has a major role and center his or her perspective as a member of a marginalized group—for example, focusing on Éowyn's experiences as a woman fighting in a war or Samwise Gamgee's perspective as the sole working-class member of the Fellowship.

Historically, Tolkien fanfiction has undertaken this work most often for two groups of characters: women and queer characters. In both cases, the reaction of the wider fanfiction community has shown this to be a fraught endeavor, with responses often outsized and mirroring the oppressive treatment faced by real-world members of those groups. Following the release of Jackson's *The Lord of the Rings* films, interest in Tolkien-based fanfiction exploded on the Internet. One particular genre was so popular that it was given its own name: the Tenth Walker story. In these stories, a highly idealized girl or young woman, often based on the author and called a self-insert, joined the Fellowship on their quest. She typically attracted the romantic interest of at least one of the book characters, and this is where the story often focused. Authors of Tenth Walker stories were typically teen girls.

Similar was the Mary Sue phenomenon. Mary Sue is a generally derogatory term that originated in *Star Trek* fandom for an idealized original female character who exerted enough influence to reshape the plot or cause characters to behave out-of-character. In the early online Tolkien fanfiction community, the use of the term Mary Sue is interesting because of how it umbrellaed very quickly until it encompassed nearly any story that involved an original female character. The presence of an original female character alone—no matter how well-written—could earn disapprobation as a Mary Sue. In reading back through message archives for Tolkien fanfiction groups in the early to mid 2000s, I encountered anxiety from authors who *wanted* to write more women in their stories but feared receiving the dreaded label of Mary Sue. Authors who did write women often took extra care to steer their characterization away from anything that suggested the traits of a Mary Sue (Walls-Thumma 2019, 26). Since a Mary Sue is, by definition, an original character who drives plot and characterization from the canon, this often led authors to write women into only passive or supporting roles.

Taking in a wider view of Western storytelling, none of this is terribly radical. After all, the idea of an ordinary (even underwhelming) boy or man discovering that he has exceptional talents and using them, in many cases, to literally save the world is a common trope in stories that have commanded the adoration of millions of fans, such as *Spider-Man* and *Harry Potter*. Nor are self-inserts inherently a byword in fiction. Many male authors write self-inserts to great acclaim. Tolkien himself wrote more than one.[1] Finally, as a teacher who works

---

1. The tale of Beren and Lúthien is the most obvious self-insert; it includes numerous parallels to the romance between Tolkien and his wife Edith (*B&L*,

with this age group, I can attest that early adolescence is a time, developmentally, when children become alive to the full breadth of possibilities in the world around them while not yet fully cognizant of its limitations—limitations too often prescribed by the demographic group they belong to. In other words, kids at this age dream big. Therefore, there was nothing culturally or developmentally unusual about the Tenth Walker phenomenon, in young women writers responding to a text they loved by making room to see themselves as characters with enough agency to shape the story.

One would not have known it from the reaction of the broader Tolkien fanfiction community. Responses to these young women's stories utilized deliberately violent language and came both from fans acting individually as well as part of organized campaigns. One such organization, called Protectors of the Plot Continuum or PPC—a group that still operates today—originated with the primary intention to mock authors of so-called "Mary Sue" stories, a genre that includes Tenth Walkers. The PPC's wiki, where the group keeps its documents, uses explicitly violent terms to describe how group members are expected to react to self-insert fanfiction written by adolescent girls. For example, the function of the group is to "hunt down and assassinate Mary Sues." Use of firearms, poisoning, and even cannibalism are identified as appropriate methods for the fictional destruction of self-insert female characters, who are further described as "like a virus or a parasite, which must be eliminated" (Protectors of the Plot Continuum 2022, "Department of Mary Sues"; Protectors of the Plot Continuum 2022, "Mary Sue").

17). The unfinished Notion Club Papers is another text that at least began as a self-insert, with Tolkien identifying the character Ramer—who happens to be a professor of Finnish—as himself. The text details the meetings of an intellectual all-male Oxford social circle patterned after the Inklings.

While the PPC mocks many genres of story, the section of their website devoted to Mary Sue stories is the only section that uses this kind of violent language, and while the PPC is clear that their violent acts are fictional, it is significant that Mary Sues are a genre where the author is the character targeted—and the woman author at that. It is hard not to see parallels between the casual deployment of violent language against this explicitly female genre and the ongoing normalization of violence against women throughout the world, particularly against adolescent girls who are seen to have transgressed aspirational or sexual limitations placed upon them.

While the PPC "merely" mocked stories, other fans went further, and sometimes threatened writers of Tenth Walker or Mary Sue stories with harm and encouraged them to commit suicide. The authors' youth was itself held up as a legitimate justification for adults attacking the creative work of children—and sometimes the children themselves.

Another genre similarly subjected to aggressive scrutiny and attack in the early online fandom was slash, a fanfiction genre where two same-sex characters are paired together romantically or sexually. Like Mary Sue, slash has its origins in the *Star Trek* fandom and, in that fandom, was a genre with decades of history before fanfiction migrated online in the early 2000s.[2] Like Mary Sue stories, within the early online Tolkien fanfiction fandom, slash fiction was singled out for censure by other fans. Here again, the canon was weaponized

---

2. Unlike Star Trek fandom, slash fiction for Tolkien fandom does not appear to have existed—or existed in extremely limited circulation—in pre-Internet fanfiction. In Anna Smol's correspondence with the fandom historian Lisa Williams and my own personal correspondence with Elwin Fortuna, the founder of the first Tolkien slashfic archive, Least Expected, neither is aware of slash fiction prior to the fandom's migration online in the late 1990s (2004, 976).

to conceal homophobic objections within the guise of textual fidelity and respect for Tolkien. While also subjected to harassment—including threats of violence—slash authors were often explicitly excluded from the mainstream fanfiction community. This era in U.S. history is littered with legislation aimed at excluding LGBTQ+ citizens from full involvement in family, social, and cultural institutions. For example, to take the issue of marriage equality, the Defense of Marriage Act was signed into law in 1996 and the first decade of the 2000s saw a rash of state laws banning same-sex marriage, with the end result that it is banned in the state constitutions or laws of thirty-five states (Povich 2022).

Slash fanfiction and slash fanfiction authors likewise faced exclusion from mainstream fandom spaces. Multiple large archives, such as Stories of Arda and Open Scrolls Archive, disallowed slash. On other archives, policies allowed for slash but also provided mechanisms for popular censorship of stories the membership didn't like. The Henneth-Annûn Story Archive's peer-review system was accused of being wielded to exclude slash stories from the archive, among other genres (Brobeck 2004). On sites like FanFiction.net, the harassment of slash authors, including using homophobic slurs and death threats, met with a shrug from site administrators, discouraging slash authors from posting there (Walls-Thumma 2019, 11). Due to open and covert exclusion of slash, and because slash authors tended to be older than the authors of Mary Sue stories and had more resources at their disposal, slash authors tended to form their own communities within the early online Tolkien fanfiction fandom. As a result, slash flourished, but these stories went unseen by fans who did not seek them out, furthering the assumption that queer characters could not exist in Middle-earth.

In early online Tolkien fanfiction, canon was often wielded against interpretations that allowed for greater representation of diverse perspectives. The sexist underpinnings of the concept of Mary Sue were rarely scrutinized because the genre was criticized under the guise of canonicity, and the result was that many authors feared writing even women who were a canonical presence in the legendarium. Fans who sought to limit, control, or censor the types of fanfiction being produced also promoted a definition of canon that expanded beyond the texts and into their perception of Tolkien's beliefs and intentions. For example, Tolkien's Catholicism, for many fans, became an element of the canon, never mind that no character within the legendarium would have identified as a Catholic. That Catholicism also narrowed to what the most conservative fans believed it to be and allowed no room for Tolkien to maintain a complex perspective beyond his religious beliefs. Thus, queer characters were marked uncanonical, and excluding fanfiction about LGBTQ+ characters became a simple matter of fidelity to the canon and not of homophobia and could not be challenged in those terms. Again and again, what some fans thought Tolkien meant or believed he intended was elevated to the status of canon where it was not open to question and where canonicity became a convenient diversion from discussions of sexism, racism, and homophobia in the legendarium and fandom.

Once again, it is worth remembering the size and diversity of the Tolkien fanfiction fandom. Certainly, there were communities that encouraged and discussed interpretations of the canon and stories featuring characters representing the full array of human diversity. However, returning to the academic view of fanfiction as a "literature of the subordinate," as transgressive, as radical, as a means to amplify the voices and experiences of marginalized people, we can see that, by and large, in the early online fandom, Tolkien fanfiction's tendency toward a definition of its canon as conservative, in the sense of limiting rather than expanding possible perspectives, foreclosed on many of those opportunities.

2 - Tolkien Fanfiction Snapshots: 2015 and 2020

In the decades following the release of Jackson's *The Fellowship of the Ring* in theaters, fans have written and posted hundreds of thousands of stories online based on Tolkien's world. The Tolkien Fanfiction Survey offers snapshots in 2015 and 2020 of how a contingent of those fans regarded the stories that they wrote and read.

In 2015, the survey asked few demographic questions. Participants were given the option to identify their age and gender. In 2020, the survey collected more extensive demographic information, including gender, age, race/ethnicity, education, and primary language. According to the 2020 survey data, Tolkien fanfiction is largely written by college-educated young women. More specifically,

- the median age of participants was twenty-seven years, but the range of participant ages spanned the ages eighteen to eighty-one. (Institutional Review Board guidelines did not allow us to collect data from participants under the age of eighteen; had we been able to, the median age would likely shift younger.)
- 73% of participants identified as female and 15% as nonbinary.
- 67% of participants had a college degree.
- 67% of participants spoke English as their first language.

The 2020 survey allowed participants to describe their race or ethnicity rather than choosing from a list of predetermined options. While this has made analyzing these data messier, as Maria and I designed the 2020 survey, including piloting it with other fans, we became increasingly aware of how our own definitions of terms like race, *person of color*, and ethnicity were skewed by our perceptions and experiences as researchers located in the U.S. (see, for example, Lamuye 2017). We ultimately decided, given the diversity of fans within the fanfiction community, to allow participants to self-describe. As a result, data for this item should not be seen as either/or. For example, that 71% of fans included the word *white* in their response does not mean that 29% of fans are Black, Indigenous, or People of Color (BIPOC). However, based on responses, Tolkien fanfiction fandom is predominantly white and Western:

- 71% self-identified as white or Caucasian without identifying another racial or ethnic group.
- 31% identified as European or as having European ancestry (e.g., Irish-American).
- 9% identified an American national origin or ancestry. Note that this includes all American nationalities, including Latino/Latina, and does not include only the United States.
- 13% included words that, in the United States, would be considered BIPOC (unless they also included the term white, e.g., "white Latina").

Again, because the fanfiction community is international, U.S. understandings of which identities would be perceived as marginalized did not necessarily hold true. Furthermore, even within the U.S., the experiences of a single identity group are far from monolithic, and we didn't want to assume marginalization—or lack thereof—based on a participant's response to any single item. Therefore, we also allowed participants to identify if and for which identities they felt marginalized. I will also use these data to show how values and behaviors related to fanfiction vary among fans. The table below shows the percentage of participants who self-identified as members of various marginalized groups.

No, I do not identify as part of a marginalized group	23%
Sexual Orientation	58%
Gender	41%
Disability/Health Status	28%
Ethnicity	10%
Religion	9%
Social Economic Status	9%
Race/Color	6%
Immigration Status	3%
Other	2%

The surveys asked fanfiction authors about whether and why they included women, BIPOC characters, and queer characters in their stories. There were two sets of survey items, assessing two possible motives for including these characters. The first can be described as representational: including characters from marginalized groups in order to present the story from a point of view missing from the original text. The second is best described using McCormack's term "reparative" (2015). These authors go a step further, not just presenting a different perspective but using their fanfiction to fix or repair an element of the story that the author sees as racist, sexist/misogynistic, or homophobic.

In both the 2015 and 2020 surveys, authors expressed a high level of interest in using their fanfiction to explore the perspectives of female characters. In 2015, 78% of authors agreed or strongly disagreed with the statement "Writing fanfiction allows me to explore the perspectives of female characters." In 2020, this increased even further to include 83% of authors. That fewer fans wished to write about women in 2015 than 2020 likely reflects the vestiges of the disfavor directed toward women characters earlier in the fandom's history. By 2015, attitudes toward women characters had changed considerably, due in a large part to efforts by fans to celebrate and encourage fanworks about women and discussions in the fandom of the sexist implications of terms like "Mary Sue." Furthermore, *The Hobbit* films brought in new fans who did not carry the baggage of the fandom's earlier history. However, the significantly higher number of authors who wrote about women in 2020 show that, even as late as 2015, the fandom still had room to grow in this area.

While it is one thing to take on the perspectives of diverse characters, to what extent are authors comfortable with, firstly, admitting that there are problems with how gender is depicted in the legendarium and then going the extra length to use their stories to correct these problems? In 2020, 63% of authors agreed or strongly agreed with the statement, "Writing fanfiction helps me to address or correct problems with gender that I see in Tolkien's books."[3] However, among authors who

---

3. The 2015 survey compiled all three marginalized groups into a single survey item about reparative motives: "Writing fan fiction helps me to correct problems with race, gender, and sexuality that I see in Tolkien's books." For the 2020 survey, we expanded this item into three separate survey items.

identified as marginalized based on gender, reparative motives are far more comfortable and common: 83% agreed or strongly agreed.

This pattern will emerge again. Fans are generally interested in representational motives of diverse characters, but some balk at regarding their fanfiction as a vehicle for repairing the problems they may see in how marginalized characters are represented in the legendarium. (Some of these fans may not believe that there are problems at all.) However, among fans who not only belong to the same group as the characters in question but perceive themselves as marginalized due to that identity, reparative motives become much more common.

The same pattern holds true for queer characters. When asked about using fanfiction to explore the perspectives of LGBTQ+ characters, fewer authors agreed with the statement, "Writing fanfiction allows me to explore the perspectives of LGBTQ+ characters," than did with the matching statement for female characters: 60% and 66% in 2015 and 2020, respectively. However, a majority of authors still agreed, and there is the same small bump from 2015 to 2020. As with writing about women, this increase likely represents the growing acceptance of slash in the mainstream fandom and the arrival of fans for whom writing about queer characters (even if those characters were not canonically queer) was an assumed function of fanfiction. When considering slash authors specifically, not surprisingly, almost all of them (92%) agreed or strongly agreed with this survey item, which makes sense since they are, by definition, writing about LGBTQ+ characters. But again, among authors who identified as marginalized based on sexual orientation, 86% agreed with this item, a significantly higher number than

---

As such, this paper will discuss only the 2020 survey results for reparative motives.

for authors in general, suggesting again that perception of marginalization motivates the creation of stories that represent people in Middle-earth similar to the marginalized group(s) to which the author belongs.

The data on race looks different, though similar patterns emerge in some places. Far fewer authors expressed interest in using fanfiction to incorporate the perspectives of characters of color: 42% in 2015 and 49% in 2020. Returning to the earlier demographic data, this is possibly explained by the relatively few fans who identify as BIPOC themselves. Only 13% of partipants described themselves using terms that suggested they may identify as BIPOC, and only 6% of participants felt marginalized based on race or color compared to 58% and 41% for sexual orientation and gender, respectively.

With gender and sexual orientation, more authors identified representational motives for their fanfiction than they did reparational motives. When writing about BIPOC characters, the opposite was true. While about half of authors used their fanfiction to represent the perspectives of BIPOC characters, 56% agreed or strongly agreed that their stories functioned to "address or correct problems with race that I see in Tolkien's books." Among BIPOC authors, this number increases to 69%. Among authors who identify as marginalized based on race or color, the number increases yet again to 78%, until it looks more like the data for gender and sexual orientation presented above.

Why are more fans comfortable writing stories with a reparational purpose toward race than simply representing the perspectives of characters of color, when the exact opposite is true of gender and sexual orientation? This likely comes back to the authors' identities coupled with the work BIPOC fans and their allies have done to draw attention to racism both in the legendarium and the wider science fiction and fantasy publishing industry. As noted above, few fanfiction authors are BIPOC, especially when compared to authors who identify as women or LGBTQ+. White fans may feel less comfortable inhabiting a perspective where they do not themselves have firsthand experience, especially as BIPOC readers have drawn attention to how inaccurate, trivialized, and stereotyped depictions of "the other" in fiction causes harm (see, for example, Singh 2009). However, these same authors may be aware of racist elements in Tolkien's legendarium—again, due to the work of BIPOC fans—and make creative choices to mitigate these elements in their fanfiction. For example, a white author might show reluctance to casually depict the perspective of an indigenous Silvan Elf of Mirkwood if she does not have time to do the research needed to ensure she represents indigenous cultures in sensitive and accurate ways and avoids stereotypes and misconceptions that harm indigenous people. This same author might be comfortable, however, in repairing Tolkien's tendency to correlate dark skin with evil actions by explicitly writing Elves, Mortals, and Hobbits as having a range of possible skin tones. In other words, reparative writing in this case may require only surface-level changes in characters' appearances rather than the deeper, more difficult work of assuming the point of view of a marginalized character.

Taken all together, the data suggest that authors often represent the experiences of characters like them, and especially when they identify as part of a marginalized group, they are motivated to not only represent those characters but repair areas where the texts fall short of complex, nonstereotyped depictions of diverse characters. Given that the treatment of marginalized groups, historically, in Tolkien-based fanfiction communities parallels their marginalization in the wider world—consider the violent reaction to women characters perceived to have transgressed "their place" or the exclusion of stories about queer characters from fandom institutions—it is little surprise that authors from marginalized groups recognize fanfiction as a locus for repairing that marginalization more readily than authors for whom it is a hypothetical.

Furthermore, it is important to consider this data within the fandom's historical context, which was not traditionally friendly to authors wishing to use their stories to expand upon the canon, much less correct it, when the implication is that Tolkien fell short in how he wrote the legendarium (Walls-Thumma 2019, 11-2). Stories that explored gender and sexuality could have been passed over by readers uninterested in the subject or who felt uncomfortable or disagreed with the implied critique of Tolkien. Again, the reaction wasn't disinterest or refusal but harassment, exclusion, threats, and fictionalized enactments of violence against those authors. As noted above, the canon was weaponized in these situations and used to silence criticism of the readers who attacked authors who wrote about women or LGBTQ+ characters: Those readers objected to the distortion of the canon, not to the presence per se of women or queer characters or characters of color, never mind that, by defining canon in conservative or limiting terms, they deliberately foreclosed upon any opportunity for meaningful inclusion of those characters. The same pattern is being enacted again today, as fanworks increasingly represent Tolkien's characters as people of color and Amazon's *The Rings of Power* adaptation cast BIPOC actors. Again, canonicity is brought out as a red herring that draws the discussion away from racist motives behind objections to more diverse representations of the characters.

Part of Tolkien's genius was that he crafted the legendarium to always invite readers to journey imaginatively beyond the people, places, and perspectives that received his focus. When Aragorn mentions going "where the stars are strange," Tolkien expands his map for readers who wish to see—and see themselves in—those lands. His presentation of his work as historical artifacts invite the reader to imagine those same people and events seen through other eyes (*FR*, 'The Council of Elrond', 278). These devices and details are equally canonical—maybe even more so—than those used to exclude diverse fans who imagine the legendarium has room for them—as it does. Survey data shows that Tolkien fanfiction writers still hold an immense regard, almost a reverence, for the canon and often for Tolkien himself. It is through a fuller understanding of what that canon includes—and who it invites into the stories it tells—that has begun to evolve.

Bibliography

Bacon-Smith, Camille, *Enterprising Women: Television Fandom and the Creation of Popular Myth*, (Philadelphia: University of Pennsylvania Press, 1992).

Brobeck, Kristi Lee, 'Under the Waterfall: A Fanfiction Community's Analysis of Their Self-Representation and Peer Review', *Refractory: A Journal of Entertainment Media*, 5 (2004) <https://refractoryjournal.net/under-the-waterfall-a-fanfiction-communitys-analysis-of-their-self-representation-and-peer-review-kristi-lee/> [accessed 20 October 2022]

De Kosnik, Abigail, *Rogue Archives: Digital Cultural Memory and Media Fandom*, (Cambridge, MA: MIT Press, 2016).

Derecho, Abigail, 'Archontic Literature: A Definition, a History, and Several Theories of Fan Fiction', in *Fan Fiction and Fan Communities in the Age of the Internet*, ed. by Karen Hellekson and Kristina Busse (Jefferson, NC: McFarland, 2006), pp. 61-78.

Gilchrist, Todd, 'Evangeline Lilly Talks Tauriel, Tolkien and Love Triangle in "Desolation of Smaug"', *CBR*, 13 December 2013, <https://www.cbr.com/evangeline-lilly-talks-tauriel-tolkien-and-love-triangle-in-desolation-of-smaug/> [accessed 20 October 2022]

Ibata, David, '"Lord" of racism? Critics view trilogy as discriminatory', *Chicago Tribune*, 12 January 2003, <https://www.chicagotribune.com/lifestyles/chi-030112epringsrace-story.html> [accessed 20 October 2022]

Jenkins, Henry, *Textual Poachers: Television Fans and Participatory Culture*, Updated Twentieth Anniversary Edn, (New York: Routledge, 2013).

Lamuye, Adebola. 'I am no "person of colour", I am a black African woman', *Independent*, 31 July 2017, <https://www.independent.co.uk/voices/phrase-people-person-of-colour-bme-black-woman-women-different-experiences-race-racism-a7868586.html> [accessed 20 October 2022]

McCormack, Una, 'Finding Ourselves in the (Un)Mapped Lands: Women's Reparative Readings of *The Lord of the Rings*', in *Perilous and Fair: Women in the Works and Life of J.R.R. Tolkien*, ed. by Janet Brennan Croft and Leslie A. Donovan (Altadena, CA: Mythopoeic Press, 2015), pp. 309-26.

Povich, Elaine, 'Without Obergefell, Most States Would Have Same-Sex Marriage Bans', *Pew Charitable Trust*, 7 July 2022, <https://www.pewtrusts. org/en/research-and-analysis/blogs/stateline/2022/07/07/without-obergefell-most-states-would-have-same-sex-marriage-bans> [accessed 20 October 2022]

Protectors of the Plot Continuum, *Department of Mary Sues*, wiki, Fandom. com, 30 June 2022, <https://ppc.fandom.com/wiki/Department_of_Mary_ Sues> [accessed 18 August 2022].
--- *Mary Sues*, wiki, Fandom.com, 9 July 2022, <https://ppc.fandom.com/ wiki/Mary_Sue> [accessed 18 August 2022]

Pugh, Sheenagh, *The Democratic Genre: Fan Fiction in a Literary Context*, (Bridgend: Seren, 2005).

Seah, Naomii, 'Why we shouldn't glorify *Lord of the Rings*', *The Spinoff*, 9 December 2021, <https://thespinoff.co.nz/society/09-12-2021/why-we-shouldnt-glorify-lord-of-the-rings> [accessed 20 October 2022]

Singh, Vandana, 'As Others See Us: More on Writing the Other', *Antariksh Yatra*, 23 May 2009, <https://vandanasingh.wordpress.com/2009/05/23/as-others-see-us-more-on-writing-the-other/> [accessed 20 October 2022]

Smol, Anna, '"Oh. . . oh. . . Frodo!": Readings of Male Intimacy in *The Lord of the Rings*', *Modern Fiction Studies*, 50.4 (2004) <https://annasmol.files. wordpress.com/2012/06/50-4smol.pdf> [accessed 20 October 2022]

Tarhiliel, 'Eowyn in the Films', *Lady of Rohan*, n.d., <http://www. ladyofrohan.com/eowyninthefilms.html> [accessed 20 October 2022]

Tolkien, J.R.R., *The Lord of the Rings*, (New York: Ballantine: 1954).
--- *The Silmarillion*, (New York: Del Rey, 1977).
--- *The Peoples of Middle-earth*, (London: HarperCollins, 1996).

Walls-Thumma, Dawn, 'Affirmational and Transformational Values and Practices in the Tolkien Fanfiction Community', *Journal of Tolkien Research*, 8.1 (2019) <https://scholar.valpo.edu/journaloftolkienresearch/vol8/iss1/6/> [accessed 20 October 2022]

Hidden Visions:
Iconographies of Alterity in Soviet Bloc
Illustrations for *The Lord of the Rings*

Joel Merriner

Alterity can be described as the "state of being other or different" however this rather simplistic definition belies the complex symbiosis of Otherness and familiarity which the term embodies (Stevenson and Waite 2011, 38). From a Tolkienian perspective, a form of East-West alterity is understood to have arisen from the geopolitical divide of the Cold War, and this divide had an appreciable impact on matters of literary translation. As confirmed by Markova (2004), because of the erroneous assumption of the Soviet Bloc censor GLAVLIT (The Main Directorate for Literary and Publishing Affairs) that *The Lord of the Rings* constituted a veiled allegory of totalitarian East versus democratic West, prospective Eastern European Tolkien translators were impelled to create abridged or hybridised versions of the novel to appease the censor.[1] Translators themselves would also often import subjective elements into their Tolkien interpretations, resulting in works created in accordance with, to quote Natalya Grigor'eva "the translator's own way of understanding, sometimes even for their own liking" (1992, 201). When encountered today these translations appear at once familiar and yet alien, particularly to the Western reader.

---

1. Olga Markova, "When Philology Becomes Ideology: The Russian Perspective on *The Lord of the Rings*", trans. Mark T. Hooker, *Tolkien Studies* 1 (2004), 163-170 (p.165).

This model of Soviet Bloc alterity also extended to encompass visual depictions of *The Lord of the Rings*, particularly those created by illustrators of 1980s translated editions from Russia and Poland. Restrictive circumstances in these states coupled with innovative, resourceful artists engendered several unique sets of imagery. Decoding the often-cryptic illustrations in these books requires an interpretive approach tailored specifically towards the understanding of *visual alterity*, which in this case can be defined as non-normative Tolkien imagery. I have identified three distinct forms of this visual alterity in Soviet Bloc Tolkien illustrations; motif borrowing, original creation and a form of semiosis or signification process referred to as dislocation.

Forms one and three, *motif borrowing*, and *dislocation* are adventures for another day. This paper is concerned with the second form of visual alterity original creation, a phenomenon typified by the incorporation of iconographies, or subject matter, new, (at the time of creation), to Tolkien illustration. Loosely speaking we can consider this to be work which does not conform to the usual neo-medieval aesthetic associated with modern Tolkien visual culture.

This paper will concentrate on the work of a trio of illustrators whose images for translations of *The Lord of the Rings* epitomise this approach. These illustrators are Jerzy Czerniawski, the Polish artist whose illustrations accompany the 1981 revised edition of Maria Skibniewska's original 1962 Polish translation *Władca Pierścieni* (published by Czytelnik); Gennadij Kalinovskij (1929-2006) Russian illustrator of Andrej Kistjakovskij and Vladimir Murav'eva's abridged 1982 Russian translation of *The Fellowship of the Ring*, *Khraniteli* ("Guardians"), published by Detskaja Literatura, and Sergei Iukhimov (1958-2016) the Ukrainian artist responsible for the illustrations in TO Izdatel's 1993 edition of Natalya Grigor'eva and Vladimir Grushetskij's famous *Vlastelin Kolets* translation.

Beginning with the 1981 Polish edition, the task of providing illustrations for this translation was given to artist and designer Jerzy Czerniawski (1947-). Prior to 1981 Czerniawski had been particularly active in Poland's flourishing field of poster design, being numbered among the country's distinct "third generation" of designers born around the time of the Second World War (Boczar 1984, 23). This third generation was seen as being more "aggressive" than their predecessors (23), and Czerniawski regularly created work that, although not explicitly political, was designed to address what Aulich and Sylvestrová refer to as the "moral, social and ethical problems" concurrent in late 1970s Poland (1999, 55). Both Czerniawski's poster design (usually promoting Eastern European counter-cultural events and student theatre productions) and illustration work at this time can be characterised by the inclusion of distinctive visual motifs, at times baffling or disturbing, but often oddly lyrical. Oppressive state control over Polish visual culture instilled in him an approach which required the encoding of meaning into seemingly disparate text-image combinations, decipherable by those familiar with the pictorial cues. This tendency towards concealment can be detected in his illustrations for *Władca Pierścieni.*

A typical example occurs in the wrap-around dust jacket design for Volume One *Wyprawa* ("Expedition"). The front panel section of the image comprises a head and shoulders depiction of Frodo with an impassive face, eyes closed, hair straggly and snaking. The back panel features an androgynous Galadriel with pale skin, visible nipples, and eyes closed with long lashes and teardrops. The head and shoulders portrait, often paired with the serene, impassive face complete with closed or open eyes is a common motif used by Czerniawski in his poster work. Examples include the student theatre posters *Room with an Ocean View* and *Lady Macbeth Mzensk* from 1978. In these images the calm face provides a neutral vessel through which various emotions or concepts triggered by the accompanying text can be visually transmitted. Avoidance of extreme facial expressions also obviates unwanted attention from those who might censor the work.

In the case of the Volume One dust jacket image, the neutral expression of Frodo meshes with aspects of the Hobbit's character. The expression becomes a tangible reference to the Hobbit's calm acceptance of his role as Ring-bearer, as demonstrated at the Council of Elrond where regardless of an "overwhelming longing" to remain in Rivendell, he volunteers to bear the Ring to Mordor (*FR*, 'The Council of Elrond', 270). In the context of such self-sacrifice and implied martyrdom, Czerniawski's serene Frodo with his long hair and beard, cloak and stylised wounds on a naked chest also evokes images of *Christ as the Man of Sorrows*, as can be seen, for instance, in Flemish artists Quentin Metsys and Colijn de Coter's archetypal 16th century oil paintings.

Another common Czerniawski poster motif identifiable in this image concerns the spherical object resting on Frodo's head. A similar design appears in *König Lear* ("King Lear") (1981), a lithographic poster created by Czerniawski for a German stage production of Shakespeare's play. In the poster image the object depicted is a small boulder resting on the head of a grey-haired and bearded man, presumably Lear. Here the boulder may be a symbol of Lear's madness, pressing down upon him in a simulacrum of the internal struggle which Waters Bennet refers to as his "storm within" (1962, 138). In the image of Frodo, the motif has a different meaning. Instead of a boulder, close inspection reveals that the object is in fact an apple, and the motif here relates to the concept of the "apple-shot," a phenomenon referred to by folklorist Stith Thompson as a "marvel" in which a "skilful marksman" is called upon to shoot an apple from a man's head (1955, 191). As a literary device the apple-shot has a long lineage, with folklore scholars citing various influential medieval sources where the feat can be observed, the preeminent example being the Swiss legend of William Tell. Here the master crossbowman is forced to shoot an apple placed on the head of his own son as punishment for refusing to bow to a representation of the tyrannical Habsburg governor Albrecht Gessler.

Folklorist Alan Dundes decodes the apple-shot as a "painless sacrificial ritual" (1991, 352-3). In the Tell story the marksman's trusting son offers himself up willingly in the knowledge that his father's skill with the crossbow will liberate them from Gessler's oppressive attentions. It is possible to hypothesise a parallel with Frodo, who despite his internal reservations takes up the role of Ringbearer willingly, trusting that others, specifically those older, wiser pseudo-father figures such as Gandalf and Elrond will show him the way to Mount Doom and, ultimately, the Ring's destruction. From the viewer's perspective, the arrangement of visual elements in Czerniawski's image facilitates this connection.

The calm expression is also evident in another illustration of Frodo featured as the endpaper image in Volume Two, *Dwie Wieże* ('The Two Towers'). This, however, depicts a Frodo rendered effectively blind and speechless by Shelob's paralysing poison. The autumnal leaves (symbols of decay) merging with his eyes and obscuring the Hobbit's mouth symbolise his loss of control, he cannot see or speak, and appears to be dead.

Power over vision, often embodied in potentially violent form is another motif common to Czerniawski's countercultural designs, for example the lithographic posters *A Tree of Desires* (1978) and *A Dream Play* (1977). Here the juxtaposition of a sharp beak and metal spike with human eyes suggests the vulnerability of the gaze in an oppressive society. This again we can see echoed in Czerniawski's Tolkien illustrations, as here in the Volume One endpaper image he presents us with Gandalf locked in combat with a Witch-King who is symbolised by an enormous crowned black bird (with a red eye that itself is a vessel for Sauron's power), which seeks to metaphorically pierce or rupture Gandalf's own eyes with his sharp beak.

I will now move on to my second example of original creation, namely the set of chapter initials created by Gennadij Kalinovskij (1929-2006) for Detskaja Literatura's *Khraniteli* in 1982. These encompass twenty-three illuminated Cyrillic letters, one per chapter plus one also for the Prologue. Each initial is rendered in a palette of blue and grey shades and consists of an enlarged version of the first letter of the opening word of the corresponding passage. Figurative and abstract elements are combined in the initials to create a design template which Kalinovskij revisits throughout the book. Zoomorphic or foliate ornamentation lends a familiar (in Tolkienian terms) faux-medieval manuscript aesthetic to many of the initials. However, it is Kalinovskij's innovative use of overlapping geometric shapes and his incorporation of Cyrillic rather than Latin script letters into the narrative fabric of the image that gives his designs their original element.

For example, take the initial from Book One, Chapter Eleven, the title of which translates as 'A Blade in the Night', equivalent to Tolkien's 'A Knife in the Dark'. This is the letter *Pe (П)* of the opening word *Пока* (*Poka*, "While"). The accompanying sentence begins with "While they were preparing to sleep," referring to the Hobbits settling for the night in the Prancing

Pony in Bree (Kistyakovskij and Murav'ev 1982, 127). Here the letter intertwines with a diamond shape containing a motif resembling a hooded face. The face has two white eyes within what appear to be grey eye sockets. When viewed in the context of the narrative up to this point, the face is easily interpreted as a Black Rider. The Riders have figured sufficiently in the story thus far that upon viewing the image, the connection between visual motif and textual character is achieved largely automatically. In this respect Kalinovskij's letter functions as a historiated initial, displaying an identifiable scene, or character from within the accompanying passage of text.

In this next image, the actual letter forms a part of the narrative illustration itself, rather than simply containing it. The letter is *Te* (*T*) of the word *Только* (*Tol'ko* "Only"), which opens Book Two Chapter Four, 'Black Abyss', (Tolkien's 'A Journey in the Dark'). The sentence begins "Only around evening in the gloomy twilight" (Kistyakovskij and Murav'ev 1982, 225). Inserted within the curls of the letter T are two glowing eyes beneath dark brows. When combined with the blue insert and central dividing line of the diamond, this feature creates the impression of a canine muzzle. Viewed holistically, the complete initial design resembles the shadowy face of a dog or a wolf. The visual-textual connection is subsequently activated when the reader encounters the Warg attack suffered by the Fellowship later in the chapter.

Kalinovskij's initial for Book One Chapter Five 'Uncovered Conspiracy' ('A Conspiracy Unmasked') depicts the letter *Che* (*Ч*) of *Что ж* (*Chto zh* "Well") which begins the line "'Well, let's hurry up' said Merry." Here the letter is simultaneously decorative, with the two zoomorphic heads, and narrative, as the two heads are readable as Merry and Pippin in their capacity during this chapter as twin conspirators plotting (with Sam) to prevent Frodo leaving the Shire without them (Kistyakovskij and Murav'ev 1982, 71). The number two at the centre of the design neatly underlines this reading, affirming the textual hobbit pairing numerically whilst also uniting their two symbolic figures visually.

I will conclude this paper by briefly examining the work of Sergei Iukhimov, an artist responsible for the creation of one hundred and twenty full colour illustrations for *The Lord of the Rings*, thirty-two of which were included in the 1993 TO Izdatel' *Vlastelin Kolets* edition. I have previously written and presented material regarding Iukhimov's intertextual borrowing and his recourse to biblical or historical sources such as hagiographic paintings and illuminated Gospel miniatures in the construction of his Tolkien illustrations. However, the iconography I am concerned with today is not rooted in this medieval sensibility, but rather stems from the stark, brutalist or clinical architectural environments of the Soviet period.

An example can be seen here with the 1988 image *In the Tomb*, which depicts the four Hobbits inside the Barrow-wight mound. Frodo stands armed with a sword, ready to strike the sinister hand which reaches for the blade laid across his friends' necks. The salient elements of the text are present, down to Sam, Merry and Pippin, laid out with crowns and shields like figures on a recumbent effigy tomb. But the background, with its geometric lines and sickly green, gleaming tiles hints at a setting that is contemporary rather than ancient.

Iukhimov says little pertaining to this form of iconography, save for a single remark made on his blog in 2009 when talking about representations of beauty, or the lack of it, in his Tolkien illustrations. "And yet," he says "about the tile. Satan apes God. He cannot create anything [beautiful] for himself. Therefore, where there is darkness there is a toilet" (Iukhimov

2009). Iukhimov is perhaps being a touch disingenuous here, as the tile aesthetic is just as able to evoke clinical environments such as psychiatric hospitals, sanitoriums, and similar medical facilities whose edifices, particularly in times of reduced accountability such as the Soviet period, might conceal hidden evils.

In *Bridge of Khazad-dûm* the tiled setting in which Gandalf confronts the Balrog is magnified to a monumental scale, befitting the location and significance of the moment. The creature, with its elaborate headgear modelled on images of the famous 7th century Sutton Hoo helmet, inhabits an architectural space similar in size and brutalist aesthetic to huge Soviet monumental installations such as the *Founders of the Bulgarian State* monument in Shumen Bulgaria where eighteen-metre-tall carved warriors emerge from a structure fashioned out of thousands of tons of concrete and steel.

In the image *Rescue of Frodo* Sam enters the cell at the top of the tower of Cirith Ungol, where the Orc Snaga has just lashed the imprisoned Frodo with a whip. Here again Iukhimov employs the tile motif creating a particularly harsh juxtaposition of hard, clinical architecture and the softer vulnerable naked body of Frodo. The predatory attitude of Snaga looming over Frodo magnifies the unease. A primary world analogue to this oppressive setting can be seen in imagery of the internal prison of the Lubyanka building, Moscow, former headquarters of the KGB, for several decades the scene of imprisonment, torture, forced transportation to labour camps and the execution of dissidents. Here tiled floors combine with thick walls, and heavy doors to create a brutalising aesthetic.

Iukhimov weaves this iconography throughout his corpus, including in this image of Frodo and Sam in Shelob's Lair (not featured in the *Vlastelin Kolets* edition), and even extending to encompass the outside landscape, as in the front cover image of Volume Two where Frodo and Sam, disguised as orcs, encounter the slave driver on the road to Isenmouthe on the plateau of Gorgoroth in Mordor. Here the road itself, a proxy for Sauron's attempts at creation, becomes a tiled floor. To reiterate Iukhimov's words, "He [Sauron] cannot create anything [beautiful] for himself. Therefore, where there is darkness there is a toilet" (Iukhimov 2009).

The three illustrators featured in this paper are united in their ability to invest their imagery with original iconographies hitherto unseen in Tolkien illustration. Jerzy Czerniawski channels the censor-baffling motifs of the Polish counter-culture poster to create cryptic Middle-earth portraits imbued with multiple meanings. Gennadij Kalinovskij's illuminated initials encapsulate ornamentation and narration in the form of Cyrillic letters. Finally, Sergei Iukhimov's stark and sinister tiled settings conjure the oppressive architecture of a totalitarian regime. To the modern viewer the work of these individuals can appear both familiar, with recognisable characters and locations, and unfamiliar, featuring visual subject matter that differs from the neo-medieval norm. However, by engaging with this alterity, it is possible to decode the clues set within the images and shed light upon three hidden visions of Middle-earth.

Bibliography

Aulich, James and Marta Sylvestrová, *Political Posters in Central and Eastern Europe, 1945 – 1995: Signs of the Times*, (Manchester: Manchester University Press, 1999).

Boczar, Danuta A., 'The Polish Poster', *Art Journal*, 44.1 (1984), 16-27.

Dundes, Alan, 'The 1991 Archer Taylor Memorial Lecture. The Apple-shot: Interpreting the Legend of William Tell', *Western Folklore*, 50. 5 (1991), 327-360.

Grigor'eva, Natalya, 'Problems of Translating into Russian', in *Proceedings of the J.R.R. Tolkien Centenary Conference 1992*, ed. by Patricia Reynolds and Glen Goodknight (Milton Keynes: The Tolkien Society, 1992), pp 200-205.

Iukhimov, Sergei, *Tolkien*, LiveJournal, 15 January 2009, < https://iukhimov. livejournal.com>.

Markova, Olga, 'When Philology Becomes Ideology: The Russian Perspective on *The Lord of the Rings*', trans. by Mark T. Hooker, *Tolkien Studies*, 1 (2004), 163-170.

Stevenson, Angus and Maurice Waite, eds. *Concise Oxford English Dictionary* 12th ed., (Oxford: Oxford University Press, 2011).

Thompson, Stith, *Motif-Index of Folk literature Vol III*, New and Enlarged Edition, (Bloomington: Indiana University Press, 1956).

Tolkien, J.R.R., *The Fellowship of the Ring*, (Wyprawa), trans. by Maria Skibniewska (Warsaw: Czytelnik, 1981).

--- *The Two Towers*, (Dwie Wieże), trans. by Maria Skibniewska (Warsaw: Czytelnik, 1981).
--- *The Fellowship of the Ring*, (Khraniteli), trans. by Andrej Kistyakovskij and Vladimir Murav'ev (Moscow: Detskaja Literatura, 1982).
--- *The Lord of the Rings*, (Vlastelin Kolets), trans. by Natalya Grigor'eva and Vladimir Grushetskij (Moscow: TO Izdatel', 1993).
--- *The Fellowship of the Ring*, (London: HarperCollins, 2011).

Waters Bennet, Josephine, 'The Storm Within: The Madness of Lear', *Shakespeare Quarterly*, 13. 2 (1962), 137-155.

Images

de Coter, Colin, *Christ as the Man of Sorrows*, 1500, oil on panel, 650 mm x 430 mm, private collection.

Czerniawski, Jerzy, *A Dream Play*, 1977, lithograph, 980 mm x 680 mm, Polish Poster Gallery.
--- *Lady Macbeth Mzensk*, 1978, lithograph, 840 mm x 590 mm, Galeria Grafiki I Plakatu.
--- *Room with an Ocean View*, 1978, lithograph, 680 mm x 980 mm, Krakow Poster Gallery.
--- *A Tree of Desires*, 1978, lithograph, 980 mm x 680 mm, Polish Poster Gallery.
--- *König Lear*, 1981, lithograph, 840 x 593 mm, Stedelijik Museum.
--- *König Lear* ("King Lear"), 1981, lithograph, 840 x 593 mm, Stedelijik Museum, Amsterdam.

Metsys, Quentin, *Christ as the Man of Sorrows*, c. 1520-1530, oil on panel, 495 mm x 370 mm, J. Paul Getty Museum.

"Something Mighty Queer": Destabilizing Cishetero Amatonormativity in the Works of Tolkien

Danna Petersen-Deeprose

Queerness, queer theory, and queer readings of literature are always controversial topics, both because of cultural prejudice and because the term "queer" itself remains nebulous and difficult to define. Despite this, recent years have begun to see an increase in scholarship discussing queerness in Tolkien's texts, often focusing on homosexuality and homoamory in *The Lord of the Rings* books, film adaptations, and fandom. While this paper draws on that scholarship, when it discusses queerness, it does not refer specifically to same-gender sex or romance, although those are of course included. Eve Sedgwick has argued that "one of the things that 'queer' can refer to [is] the open mesh of possibilities, gaps, overlaps, dissonances and resonances, lapses and excesses of meaning when the constituent elements of anyone's gender, of anyone's sexuality, aren't made (or *can't be* made) to signify monolithically" (1993, 1). That mesh is what this paper sets out to explore. Drawing on intersectional feminist and postmodern queer theories, I will examine Tolkien's depictions of characters, relationships, ways of loving, and ways of existing that challenge contemporary cishetero amatonormative structures and assumptions.

To clarify some terminology, the term "cishetero" refers to the combination of compulsory heterosexuality, which excludes queer orientations, and compulsory cisgenderism—

that is, the idea that everyone's gender must align with their biological assigned sex.[1] The term "amatonormativity" refers to the widespread "assumptions that a central, exclusive, amorous relationship is normal for humans, in that it is a universally shared goal, and that such a relationship is normative, in that it *should* be aimed at in preference to other relationship types" (Brake 2012, 88).

Alexander Doty notes that "[i]t is arrogant to insist that all non-blatantly queer-coded characters must be read as straight—especially in cases [...] where all we have is narrative silence on the subject of certain characters' sexuality" (2010, 12). Certainly there is no explicit homosexuality in Tolkien, but there is not a great deal of explicit heterosexuality, either. Rather, we see example after example of characters who form non-heterosexual partnerships, transcend traditional gender categorization, and develop non-normative families that, while not necessarily homosexual, are deeply queer.

Both Bilbo and Frodo disrupt the cisheteronormative culture of the Shire: "The houses and the holes of Shire-hobbits were often large, and inhabited by large families. *Bilbo and Frodo Baggins were as bachelors very exceptional*" (my emphasis, *FR*, 'Concerning Hobbits', 9–10). In *Unfinished Tales* (1980), Gandalf says, "[Bilbo] had never married. [...] I guessed he wanted to remain 'unattached' for some reason deep down which he did not understand himself—or would not acknowledge for it alarmed him" (331). The implications of this statement are

---

1. Valerie Rohy and Christopher Vaccaro, among others, "remind us that the anachronistic use of contemporary terms such as 'heterosexuality', 'homosexuality', 'homoeroticism', and even 'friendship', 'love', and 'desire' can be simultaneously problematic and potentially productive" (Vaccaro 2), and I will approach these terms with caution. My purpose is not to prove the existence of any of these within the works of Tolkien, but rather to demonstrate the general lack of those distinct categories in Middle-earth.

extremely queer: there is some deep-seated reason, difficult to understand and too alarming to be acknowledged, that renders Bilbo unwilling or unable to take a wife. Bilbo further upsets the order by adopting an heir, a controversial choice given that "all Hobbits [are] clannish and reckon up their relationships with great care" (10). It is certainly seen as controversial by the other hobbits: the opening pages of *The Fellowship of the Ring* (1954) are devoted to a discussion in the local pub about Bilbo's adoption of Frodo, whether or not Frodo actually counts as a Baggins, and how it must have been a "nasty shock for those Sackville-Baggins" (30), Bilbo's would-be biological heirs. But ultimately this disruption is positive, because Bilbo's non-normative adoptive family of bachelors is the only reason the Ring is destroyed.

The Ring, moreover, is carried to Mount Doom by two male hobbits whose relationship is deeply intimate, both emotionally and physically. When Sam rescues Frodo, naked and tortured by orcs, Frodo lies "back in Sam's gentle arms, closing his eyes. [...] Sam felt he could sit like that in endless happiness" (*RK*, 'The Tower of Cirith Ungol', 218–9). Later, as they rest on their approach to Mount Doom, Sam "groped for Frodo's hand. It was cold and trembling [...] and lying down he tried to comfort Frodo with his arms and body" (258).

These are just two of many examples of their intimacy. This relationship has been discussed at length by other scholars,[2]

---

2. See, among others, Craig, David M., "'Queer lodgings': Gender and Sexuality in *The Lord of the Rings*', *Mallorn: The Journal of the Tolkien Society*, 38 (2001), 11–8; Smol, Anna. "'Oh. . . Oh. . . Frodo!": Readings of Male Intimacy in *The Lord of the Rings*', *MFS Modern Fiction Studies*, 50.4 (2004), 949–79; and Vaccaro, Christopher. "'Dyrne Langað": Secret Longing and Homo-Amory in Beowulf and J.R.R. Tolkien's *The Lord of the Rings*.' *Journal of Tolkien Research*, 6.1 (2018) <https://scholar.valpo.edu/journaloftolkienresearch/vol6/iss1/6>.

so I will not beleaguer the point. Instead, I would like to call on Ela Przybylo's discussion of Audre Lorde's seminal essay "Uses of the Erotic" (1978):

> Writing against what [Lorde] calls the "superficially erotic"—or what we might also think of as the codification of intimacy through the regime of sexuality—Lorde opens up space for a deep intimacy that is not reliant only on sex and sexuality for meaning but that finds satisfaction in a myriad of other activities and relationships to the self and to others. (2019, 22)

What we see between Frodo and Sam is precisely this deep intimacy that does not rely on sex for meaning (though it can leave open the possibility of sex, as Lorde's conception of the erotic can, but does not necessarily, fuel sexual desire). As David Craig argues, "The intimacy and love between Frodo and Sam is the moral and emotional heart of the story which is capable of saving the world from evil" (2001, 17).

There are those who contend that this relationship is not queer because it represents close male bonds formed during World War I. But that reading ignores the fact that those real-world close male bonds were frequently very queer. Some did involve sex, and others involved emotional and physical intimacy that, while nongenital, would defy contemporary understandings of heteronormativity: "to discuss intense same-sex relations during war, we must introduce a different and less distinctly sexualized array of emotional intensities and bodily sensations, a continuum of nongenital tactile tenderness that goes beyond strict gender divisions, sexual binaries, or identity politics" (Das 2002, quoted in Smol 2004, 255).

Even after the quest, the intimacy between Frodo and Sam does not end but evolves to include Rose Cotton. Sam and Rose move in with Frodo when they get married, and together the two of them settle to name their first child "Frodo", in his honour (*RK*, 'The Grey Havens', 371). When they ultimately decide against that name because the baby is a girl, Frodo is the one who names her, specifically choosing "a flower name like Rose" (371). Frodo makes them his heirs and chooses the names for their next four children as well (376). There is nothing heteronormative about this arrangement, this family. Ultimately, Frodo cannot remain in the Shire, and Sam does not feel that he can leave yet, though he is "sorrowful at heart" (377). We learn in the appendices, however, that he eventually does (*RK*, Appendix B, 470). When it comes to the end of his story, Sam's love and desire for Frodo persist. I do not mean to subordinate Sam's love for Rose and the family that he builds with her, but rather to demonstrate that this relationship, between Frodo and Sam and all three of them, whether or not it includes sex, transcends any concept of compulsory hetero amatonormativity.

This type of non-normative partnership appears repeatedly: Beleg's unfailing devotion to Túrin; Maedhros and Maglor, brothers raising foundling children; Beorn with his family of animal companions; the list goes on. Perhaps the most obvious other example is Legolas and Gimli. Compulsory amatonormativity puts forth the idea that people are either "just friends" or "more than friends," but Legolas and Gimli's relationship challenges the notion that friendship is subordinate to romantic love and that a life partner must be a sexual and romantic partner. Appendix A specifies the "great love that grew between [Gimli] and Legolas" (*RK*, Appendix A, III, 447), and it is said that Gimli goes with Legolas across the sea

> because of their great friendship, greater than any that has been between Elf and Dwarf. If this is true, then it is strange indeed: that a Dwarf should be willing to leave Middle-earth for any love, or that the Eldar should receive him. (447)

The strangeness is perhaps understated. Gimli is mortal and mortals are not allowed to enter the realm beyond the sea. The only exceptions to that rule have been the Ring-bearers, who are granted special dispensation, and Tuor, because he marries an elf: "in after days it was sung that Tuor alone of mortal Men was numbered among the elder race, and was joined with the Noldor, whom he loved; and his fate is sundered from the fate of Men" (*Silmarillion*, 294).

Of course, the appendix also states that "it is said that Gimli went also out of desire to see again the beauty of Galadriel" (*RK*, Appendix A, III, 447), which offers a more heteronormative explanation. No admiration of a lady's beauty can negate the queerness of this partnership, though. We do not see between Legolas and Gimli the physical tenderness that exists between Frodo and Sam, but we do see them elevate friendship to the level usually reserved for romance: lifelong partnership and mutual commitment that stretches beyond the edges of the world and into immortality. This type of relationship dismantles compulsory hetero amatonormativity by simply bypassing it and presenting a different model of family.

Throughout Tolkien's writing, same-gender love and friendship are a recurring motif. He specifically discusses the relationship between friendship and romantic or sexual love among elves. A footnote in *The Nature of Middle-earth* (2021) explains:

> *Love*, which Men might call "friendship" [...] is represented by √*mel*. This was primarily a motion of inclination of the *fëa*, and therefore could occur between persons of the same sex or different sexes. [...] Such persons were often called *melotorni* "love-brothers" and *meletheldi* "love-sisters".
>
> The "desire" for marriage and bodily union was represented

by √*yer*; but this never in the uncorrupted occurred without "love" √*mel*, nor without the desire for children. This element was therefore seldom used except to describe occasions of its dominance in the process of courting and marriage. The feelings of lovers desiring marriage, and of husband and wife, were usually described by √*mel*. This "love" remained, of course, permanent after the satisfaction of √*yer* in "the Time of the Children". ('Time-scales', fn2)

Tolkien thus draws very little distinction between love between friends and love between spouses. The same word is used for both in Quenya, with a separate word used specifically for sexual desire. The book goes on to describe how the "Time of the Children," the developmental stage during which elves procreate, "was in normal lives a continuous series, occupying some 12 to 60 years" ('Time-scales'). In the lifespan of an elf, this is quite a short period of time, and Tolkien's essay 'Of the Laws and Customs Among the Eldar' describes how although "[t]he union of love is indeed to them great delight and joy," "with the exercise of the power the desire soon ceases, and the mind turns to other things" (*Morgoth*, 'Myth's Transformed'). Therefore √*yer* plays a relatively small, though important, role, and √*mel* is felt between elves of any gender.[3] Although sexual

3. Although the above quotation seems to affirm the possibility of homoromantic love, the assertion that √*yer* "never in the uncorrupted occurred [...] without the desire for children" (fn2) suggests, of course, that there could be no homosexual sex—or, for that matter, any sex at all for childless couples, given the implications in 'Of the Laws and Customs Among the Eldar' that procreation for elves is a force of will, to be chosen and exercised deliberately (*Morgoth*, 'Myths Transformed'). However, the term "uncorrupted" is vague and undefined. Could not many of the elves in Beleriand and Eriador, such as those who participated in the kinslayings, be considered corrupted? Are the Avari corrupted because they refused the call of the Valar? Are all elves corrupted simply as a consequence of living in Arda Marred? Exactly what it

desire is held apart, romantic love and platonic love appear to be one and the same, and √*mel* between elves of the same gender is so powerful and such an important part of the culture that there are specific Quenya words to describe it: *melotorni* and *meletheldi*. Assuming that these concepts are known also to Sylvan and Sindarin elves, Legolas's love for Gimli is unusual not for its intensity or for the gender of its recipient, but only because it exists between an elf and a dwarf rather than between two elves. Likewise, Beleg's love for Túrin and the devotion between Fingon and Maedhros are not exceptional. Same-gender love, it would seem, is not subordinate to heterosexual love.

Tolkien's works also include several characters who, like Bilbo, never enter into any partnership, same-sex or otherwise. Haleth, chief of the Haladin, for example, refuses to wed: "Haleth was proud, and unwilling to be guided or ruled, and most of the Haladin were of like mood. [...] Haleth remained their chief while her days lasted, but she did not wed, and the headship afterwards passed to Haldan son of Haldar her brother" (*Silmarillion*, 170). Haleth's decision is left uncontested and never has negative implications or repercussions for her or for her people. Even among the Valar, marriage is not an option chosen by all. Both Ulmo and Nienna remain unpartnered, and this is not presented as a source of surprise or disruption.

---

is that allows a corrupted *fëa* to experience lust is also unclear. Can an elf feel lust because they are corrupt, or are they corrupt because they feel lust? One way or another, if a "corrupted" elf can experience √*yer* without the desire for children, then there is endless possibility for homosexual sex in Middle-earth. Furthermore, even heterosexual elves will only have sex a handful of times, given that "[t]here were seldom more than four children in any house, and the number grew less as ages passed" (*Morgoth*, 'Myths Transformed'), and otherwise the love between them will not differ from that between the *melotorni* and *meletheldi*.

They are both forces of good, untainted by any evil: Ulmo is the Vala who most aids the elves during their long war with Melkor, while Nienna collaborates with Yavanna to make the Two Trees, and "all those who wait in Mandos cry to her, for she brings strength to the spirit and turns sorrow to wisdom" (19). For the Valar, unlike for Hobbits, remaining unpartnered is not negative or destabilizing.

Queerness does not always take the form of wholesome families and partnerships, however. Frodo, Bilbo, and Sméagol's apparent asexuality, for example, does seem to be tied to the evil of the Ring. Other characters who resist or are uninterested in compulsive heterosexuality are also frequently those who are evil or weak. Boromir is explicitly described as "taking no wife and delighting chiefly in arms" (*RK*, Appendix A, I, iv, 413), a description that can be read to imply either asexuality or homosexuality, and he is the man who gives in to the power of the Ring. As Ty Rosenthal states, "[c]haracters who do not desire marriage and/or sex, even though they might, such as Boromir and Frodo, have something wrong with them" (2004, 36). And there is one character in particular whose non-normative relationships are especially destructive: Sauron.

Like Frodo and so many others, Sauron enters into intense relationships with other male characters. Unlike them, he is such a powerful character that his actions and relationships are destabilizing not just thematically or for a small society like the Shire, but for Middle-earth at large.

> In the beginning of Arda Melkor seduced [Sauron] to his allegiance, and he became the greatest and most trusted of the servants of the Enemy, and the most perilous, for he could assume many forms, and for long if he willed he could still appear noble and beautiful. (*Silmarillion*, 341)

Sauron is thus seduced away from the good Valar and comes to serve Morgoth, whom he "adore[s]" (*Morgoth*, 'Myth's Transformed'), with obsessive devotion that lasts even after Morgoth's overthrow. In *The Return of the King* (1955), Gandalf says, "Other evils there are that may come; for Sauron is himself but a servant or emissary" ('The Last Debate', 178), implying that Sauron continues to act as a servant of Morgoth, more than six thousand years after Morgoth's defeat. Sauron "is led away from his *original and correct allegiances* to the Valar and Iluvatar" (my emphasis, Alberto 2017, 70). Whether or not this adoration is erotic, this rhetoric of loving the wrong person in defiance of God is a deeply queer one. Especially because of where it leads.

Morgoth's original seduction eventually turns Sauron himself into a seducer who lures other male characters into evil (and more explicitly queer) relationships; queerness here is presented as contagious, as a dangerous cycle. In the Second Age, Sauron becomes a clear example of the archetypal queer villain. He demonstrates a pattern of taking on a fair body and seducing powerful male figures to achieve his ends. I would argue that the relationships Sauron pursues with Celebrimbor and Ar-Pharazôn are both openly coded as homoerotic.

Sauron is able to seduce the elves of Eregion, including the great smith Celebrimbor, Lord of Eregion, who will eventually forge the Three Rings of the Elves. Sauron accomplishes this seduction because of his ability to take on a fair form: he comes to Eriador "wearing the fairest form that he could contrive" (*UT*, 236). Together they forge the Rings of Power, which go on to destabilize the entire known world. When Celebrimbor learns the truth about Sauron's intentions, he hides the Rings and Sauron kills him: "In black anger [Sauron] turned back to battle; and bearing as a banner Celebrimbor's body hung upon a pole, shot through with Orc-arrows" (238). This image of a male figure strung up pierced full of arrows is clear Saint Sebastian iconography.

Saint Sebastian has been a recognized symbol of male homosexual desire for centuries, and "[w]ith impassioned if veiled enthusiasm, late-Victorian writers [...] submitted to images of St. Sebastian as a coded means of articulating same-sex desire" (Kaye, 1999, 291). This coding of Saint Sebastian as a symbol of homoeroticism only grew in the following decades (Kaye 1995, 24), though Kaye notes that "such implications could only be oblique within a Victorian context" (1999, 293). For Tolkien, too, any reference to sexuality, straight or queer, remains oblique. The implications here, however, are fairly blatant. Celebrimbor is beguiled by a fair male figure who shares dangerous secrets, and he ends up on a pole, shot through with arrows. Nor do the parallels between Celebrimbor and Saint Sebastian end with that iconography. They extend to the relationship between Sebastian and the Roman emperor who has him shot:

There is a traditional recount of Emperor Diocletian "examining the culprit himself and saying, 'Why hast thou thus rebelled against me, who honored thee above all thy comrades?'" (According to Bell, Sebastian replied that, while he had prayed for Diocletian, he could not worship Roman "idols of wood and stone.") Yet if Victorian writers saw the devotion between Sebastian and Diocletian as having a deep emotional dimension, it was inescapably the case that the Emperor had turned against his young charge. The myth of Sebastian was one of adoration cruelly refused or severed—a counter-romance of same-sex relations. (293)

Similarly, Sauron is initially a teacher and mentor to Celebrimbor and the elves of Eregion, who "learned of him many things, for his knowledge was great. [...] Sauron guided their labours" (*Silmarillion*, 344). It is Celebrimbor who finally perceives Sauron's "evil purposes" (*FR*, 'The Council of Elrond', 317) and hides the Rings of Power. Thereafter, "[w]hen Sauron learned of the repentance and revolt of Celebrimbor his disguise fell and his wrath was revealed" (*UT*, 237). Tolkien weaves careful references to various religions and mythologies through his entire Legendarium. As a Catholic, he would recognize Saint Sebastian's iconography, and as a distinguished scholar of the arts, he would likely understand the cultural significance thereof. Like that between Saint Sebastian and Diocletian, the relationship between Celebrimbor and Sauron represents "a counter-romance of same-sex relations" (Kaye 1999, 293).

Soon after, Sauron enters into a relationship with the human king Ar-Pharazôn. He again assumes a fair form, voluntarily allows Ar-Pharazôn to take him captive,[4] and "seduces the King" (*RK*, Appendix B, 450):

> Sauron [...] humbled himself before Ar-Pharazôn and smoothed his tongue [...] Yet such was the cunning of his mind and mouth that ere three years had passed he had become closest to the secret counsels of the King; for flattery sweet as honey was ever on his tongue [...] Then Ar-Pharazôn, being besotted [...] hearkened to Sauron; and he began to ponder in his heart how he might make war upon the Valar. (*Silmarillion*, 324–9)

Through these techniques Sauron convinces the King to first perform human sacrifice and then go to war against the Valar,

---

4. "Sauron was not in fact overthrown personally: his 'captivity' was voluntary" (*Morgoth*, 'Myths Transformed').

rousing the wrath of Ilúvatar, who responds by smiting the island nation with a terrible wave: "Númenor went down into the sea, with all its children and its wives and its maidens and its ladies" (*Silmarillion*, 344–5). Specifically, it is the children, wives, and maidens who suffer from this queering of Númenórian aristocracy.

Celebrimbor and Ar-Pharazôn are the most blatant examples of this queer-coding of Sauron, but there are others. For example, "[w]hen Thangorodrim was broken and Morgoth overthrown, Sauron put on his fair hue again and did obeisance to Eönwë the herald of Manwë" (241). Sauron succeeds in convincing Eönwë that he has repented, and although Eönwë does not have the authority to fully pardon him, he does not destroy his body or take him prisoner, instead leaving Sauron alone in Middle-earth. This is only a small moment, but it reinforces the modus operandi that we will see from Sauron throughout the Second Age: he does not succeed through strength of arms, but rather by taking on a beautiful form and flattering a powerful male figure.

These two oppositional representations of queerness must be read in balance. My argument is not that Tolkien universally champions queerness, but rather that queer characters and queer relationships are woven deeply into the fabric of his world and stories. This can be elucidated by comparing two relationships between servant and master. One of them is an intensely destructive, violent relationship that results almost solely in death and destruction; the other is a supportive, trusting, mutually caring relationship that results in salvation of the world itself.

Indeed, Sam's devotion to his "master" Frodo (*FR*, 'A Short Cut to Mushrooms', 109 and throughout) can be compared to Sauron's devotion to his "Master" Morgoth (*Morgoth*, 'Myths Transformed'): "He [Sam] knew now where his place was and had been: at his master's side [...] Back he ran down the steps, down the path towards Frodo" (*TT*, 'The Choices of Master Samwise', 430). Thus too Sauron "walked behind [Morgoth] on the same ruinous path down into the Void" (*Silmarillion*, 24). These are both depictions of world-changing, undying same-gender love and devotion. *The Lord of the Rings* ends with a trio of tidy marriages, but the driving force behind the main storylines—behind the actions of the villain and of the saviours—is this love that is not heterosexual or homosexual or anything that can be categorized so neatly.

Ideas of sexuality and relationships between the sexes are intricately related to ideas of gender. Like relationship categories, traditional gender and sex categories are also destabilized in the works of Tolkien. This is evident in the very world, in the ways that the various peoples of Middle-earth all demonstrate different models of gender. The dwarves "have beards from the beginning of their lives, male and female alike; nor indeed can their womenkind be discerned by those of other race" (*Jewels*, 205). This is because the dwarves were not created by Ilúvatar but by the Vala Aulë. In one version, it is explained that Ilúvatar "would not amend the work of Aulë, and Aulë had yet made only things of male form, therefore the women of the Dwarves resemble their men more than all other [...] races" (211).[5] Physical sexual characteristics appear fairly immaterial to gender for dwarves and, it would seem, for Ilúvatar as well, as he did not see a need to amend them.

Similarly, there is "less difference in strength and speed between elven-men and elven-women [...] than is seen among mortals" (*Morgoth*, 'Of the Laws and Customs Among the

---

5. Tolkien changed his mind several times about the creation of the dwarves. In other versions, Aulë makes dwarf women as well as dwarf men, but they still all have beards.

Eldar'). When we first meet Galadriel and Celeborn in *The Fellowship of the Ring*, they are described in equivalent terms: "Very tall they were, and the Lady no less tall than the Lord; and they were grave and beautiful. They were clad wholly in white; and the hair of the Lady was of deep gold, and the hair of the Lord Celeborn was of silver long and bright" ('The Mirror of Galadriel', 465). Galadriel's mother-name is "Nerwen," which literally means "man-maiden," characterising her as a masculine figure because of her height and force of will (*Peoples*, 'The Shibboleth of Fëanor'). On the other hand, male elves in general would often appear feminine or gender-nonconforming by contemporary Western standards, with their long hair braided with gold, their jewellery, and their beardless faces.[6] As John Miller observes, all elves, regardless of sex, are coded as feminine: "Like the trees themselves, elves are feminine in appearance: slender, beautiful, and resilient" (2016, 38). We get very few physical descriptions of Legolas, but we know he is "tall as a young tree, lithe" (*Lost Tales II*, 'The History of Eriol or Ælfwine and the End of the Tales'), and "fair of face beyond the measure of Men" (*RK*, 'The Battle of the Pelennor Fields', 139) with "fair" and "slender" hands and "bright elven-eyes" (*TT*, 'The Riders of Rohan', 27, 43). Miller further argues that "[r]ace [...] becomes a way of inscribing gender. The other races of Middle-earth represent alternatives to the version of masculinity embodied in the race of Men" (2016, 136). The elves, in particular, present an alternative ideal of masculinity. We might say that all dwarves are masculine and all elves are feminine, but even those terms cannot really be applied to these peoples who have fundamentally different experiences of gender and gender presentation.

6. There are rare examples of elves with beards, but they are extremely uncommon. Only two are ever mentioned by name: Círdan and Mahtan.

Further, Tolkien explicitly states that for elves, biological sex and gender identity are separate: "*fëar* of the Elves are of their nature male and female, and not their *hrondor* only" (*Morgoth*, 'Of the Laws and Customs Among the Eldar'). By making it clear that gender lies not in the body, Tolkien breaks with gender essentialism and leaves open the possibility of transgender elves. I would argue that the phrasing male *and* female, not male *or* female, also allows the possibility of both non-binary and intersex elves. In fact, in one of his earliest Elven languages, Tolkien even created the word "gwegwin" to mean "hermaphrodite" ('The Gnomish Lexicon', 44); evidently Tolkien did imagine intersex elves and deliberately included them in his language, eschewing with a biological sexual binary.

This gender/body divide is also present in the Ainur. They are essentially bodiless, although they can take on a physical form if they choose, and they have an innate internal sense of gender. If they choose to take on a physical body, then they

> take upon them forms some as of male and some as of female; for that difference of temper they had even from their beginning, and it is but bodied forth in the choice of each, not made by the choice. (*Silmarillion*, 11)

Thus in the very opening pages of the Ainulindalë, the essentialist idea that body determines gender is rejected. Furthermore, the Ainur can take any shape they like, or no shape at all, and are not bound by any sexual binary. For example, the Vala Yavanna at times takes the form of a woman, "but at times she takes other shapes. Some there are who have seen her standing like a tree under heaven, crowned with the Sun; and from all its branches there spilled a golden dew" (*Silmarillion*, 18). There is endless possibility of Ainur whose "temper" is non-binary or fluid, and as with elves, this separation of gender from biology leaves open those possibilities. Either way, the Ainur have the innate ability to change their bodies or throw them off at will, depending on their current desires and temperament.

Like the elves and dwarves, hobbits are ambiguously gendered. They have high voices and beardless faces, and they're *small*. The adults appear as children and they possess the androgyny of children. And of course, any discussion of gender nonconformity within Tolkien would be incomplete without mention of Éowyn. The Witch-King says that no "living man" can hinder him (*RK*, 'The Battle of the Pelennor Fields', 129), and he is killed by Éowyn and Merry—neither of whom is a man. In fact, when Pippin is called a "man," he indignantly replies, "Man! Indeed not! I am a hobbit" (8). Here we have two different ideas of what it means to be a man: species and gender. Éowyn and Merry might each call the other a man, but neither would identify as such. The Rohirrim want to leave behind everyone not-man, but it is specifically the not-men, maybe-men, depending-on-definition-men who defeat the lord of the Nazgûl.

There are those who read Éowyn's arc as reinforcing gender ideologies, arguing that when she falls in love with Faramir, "she begins fully to return to her true nature as a woman. [...] The references to healing and growing show that she has embraced the womanly role assigned for her" (Craig 2001, 14). But I would argue that almost all of *The Lord of the Rings* heroes choose a life of healing and growing. Sam travels the Shire planting trees. Aragorn comes into his kingship not on the battlefield but in the Houses of Healing and claims it by planting a tree. And Éowyn goes to Ithilien *with* Faramir, who does "not love the bright sword for its sharpness, nor the arrow for its swiftness, nor the warrior for his glory [but] only that which they defend" (*TT*, 'The Window on the West', 346), and it is he who suggests that together they "dwell in fair Ithilien and there make a garden" (*RK*, 'The Steward and the King', 292). Within Tolkien's world, these are not attributes that signify a womanly role. That Éowyn is happy to exist as a woman when she finds a place where that can be a gift rather than a cage does not detract from the fact that her journey is one of challenging essentialist ideas of what a woman is, what a man is, and what they can and cannot do.

Ultimately, Tolkien presents a myriad of different ways of experiencing gender, sexuality, and family—sometimes cast as positive, sometimes negative, but always complicated and subjective. Female dwarves have beards and are indistinguishable from male dwarves, while male elves have long hair, lithe physiques, and smooth cheeks. Sauron pursues non-normative relationships with other male characters, which destabilize the world at large and lead to millennia of death and destruction, while Frodo and Sam's non-normative relationship counters that, saves the world, and destroys the corrupting power of the Ring.

Thus Tolkien's fiction is filled with queer relationships and characters, as well as a complicated approach to gender and sex that leaves space for transgender, non-binary, and intersex characters. What we might read as gender nonconformity is, in many ways, normative in Middle-earth, and relationships that we might call non-normative are integral to the redemption of the world. Certainly Frodo, Boromir, Sauron and others represent non-normative sexuality and gender in ways that can be read as negative, and there is a fair degree of compulsory hetero amatonormativity brought in at the end of *The Lord of the Rings*. But there are also plenty of cisheteronormative villains, and even Sauron's queer relationships are complex; his ability to "admire" Morgoth is described as "a shadow of good" within him (*Morgoth*, 'Myth's Transformed'). So while on the surface Tolkien's fiction can reinforce gender norms and compulsory cishetero amatonormativity, beneath the surface, it in fact destabilizes both. In Arda, Tolkien has envisioned a world with a wide range of diverse sexual, romantic, familial, and gender categories. And as the Gaffer would say, "If that's being queer, then we could do with a bit more queerness in these parts" (*FR*, 'A Long-Expected Party', 31).

Bibliography

Alberto, Maria, '"It Had Been His Virtue, And Therefore Also the Cause of His Fall": Seduction as a Mythopoeic Accounting for Evil in Tolkien's Work', *Mythlore*, 35.2 (2017), 63–80.

Brake, Elizabeth, *Minimizing Marriage: Marriage, Morality, and the Law*, (Oxford: Oxford University Press, 2012).

Chance, Jane, *Tolkien, Self and Other: 'This Queer Creature'*, (London: Palgrave MacMillan, 2017).

Craig, David M., '"Queer lodgings": Gender and Sexuality in *The Lord of the Rings*', *Mallorn: The Journal of the Tolkien Society*, 38 (2001), 11–18.

Das, Santanu, '"Kiss me, Hardy": Intimacy, Gender, and Gesture in World War I Trench Literature', *Modernism/Modernity*, 9 (2002), 51–74.

Doty, Alexander, *Flaming Classics: Queering the Film Canon*, (Abingdon: Routledge, 2010).

Kaye, Richard A, '"Intangible Arrows": Stevens, St. Sebastian, and the Search for the Real', *Wallace Stevens Journal*, 19.1 (1995), 19–35.
--- '"Determined Raptures": St. Sebastian and the Victorian Discourse of Decadence', *Victorian Literature and Culture*, 27.1 (1999), 269–303.

Miller, John, 'Mapping Gender in Middle-earth', *Mythlore*, 24.2 (2016), 133–52.

Przybylo, Ela, *Asexual Erotics: Intimate Readings of Compulsory Sexuality*, (Columbus: Ohio State University Press, 2019).

Rohy, Valerie, 'On Fairy Stories', *MFS Modern Fiction Studies*, 50.4 (2004), 927–48.

Rosenthal, Ty, 'Warm Beds Are Good: Sex and Libido in Tolkien's Writing', *Mallorn: The Journal of the Tolkien Society*, 42 (2004), 35–42.

Sedgwick, Eve, *Tendencies*, (Durham: Duke University Press, 1993).
Smol, Anna, '"Oh. . . Oh. . . Frodo!": Readings of Male Intimacy in *The Lord of the Rings*', *MFS Modern Fiction Studies*, 50.4 (2004), 949–79.

Tolkien, J.R.R., *Unfinished Tales: of Númenor and Middle-Earth*, ed. Christopher Tolkien, (Crow's Nest: Allen & Unwin, 1990).

--- *The Book of Lost Tales Part 2*, ed. Christopher Tolkien, (London: HarperCollins, 1994). Ebook.

--- 'The Gnomish Lexicon', *Parma Eldalamberon* 11, ed. Christopher Gilson et al, (East Lansing: Mythopoeic Society, 1995), pp. 17–75.

--- *Morgoth's Ring*, ed. Christopher Tolkien, (London: HarperCollins, 1995). Ebook.

--- *The Peoples of Middle-earth*, ed. Christopher Tolkien, (Crow's Nest: Allen & Unwin, 1996). Ebook.

--- *The Hobbit*, (London: HarperCollins, 1998).

--- *The Return of the King*, (London: HarperCollins, 1999).

--- *The Silmarillion*, ed. Christopher Tolkien, (London: HarperCollins, 1999).

--- *The Two Towers*, (London: HarperCollins, 1999).

--- *The Fellowship of the Ring*, (London: HarperCollins, 1999).

--- *The War of the Jewels*, ed. Christopher Tolkien, (London: HarperCollins, 2002). Ebook.

--- *The Nature of Middle-earth*, ed. Carl F. Hostetter, (London: HarperCollins, 2021). Ebook.

Vaccaro, Christopher. '"Dyrne Langað": Secret Longing and Homo-Amory in Beowulf and J.R.R. Tolkien's *The Lord of the Rings*', *Journal of Tolkien Research*, 6.1, 2018 <https://scholar.valpo.edu/journaloftolkienresearch/vol6/iss1/6>.

The Invisible Other: Tolkien's Dwarf-Women and the 'Feminine Lack'

Sara Brown

J.R.R. Tolkien's world of Middle-earth presents the reader with changing landscapes, diverse geographical features, disparate cultures, and many different types of creatures – some human, some humanoid and some that resemble neither. In many ways, the reader's journey is both across and through species, as these inform an understanding of the cultural tensions and the conflicts that exist within Middle-earth. Throughout the legendarium, these diverse species articulate their differences through culturally-specific mores, such as gender roles and attitudes to procreation, as well as through a consideration of their genesis.

Tolkien's portrayal of female characters in *The Lord of the Rings* is undeniably problematic. Galadriel may be powerful in her own right as one of the last remaining of the ancient Noldor who rebelled against the Valar, and keeper of Nenya, the ring of Adamant, protecting Lothlórien against encroaching evil. She is also, however, idealised in her beauty and in her effect on the (male) characters around her. Arwen is revealed only in relation to Aragorn's story, remaining at home to sew banners while the hero battles to save Middle-earth until they can be reunited and married. She is required to sacrifice her one power – her immortality – to be with the one she loves and is almost an afterthought in terms of her agency within the narrative, appearing only in the Appendices. Goldberry is connected to the power of nature but is depicted primarily through her relationship to male characters. She is Tom Bombadil's wife and the 'River daughter'; her main role is to be welcoming, provide care and comfort, and produce food for the table. Éowyn begins her story as a shield maiden of Rohan, but ultimately settles for the roles of wife, mother, and healer. Rosie Cotton is invisible until the final chapters, when she is revealed as Sam's fiancée, then wife, then mother to his children – his 'reward' after returning from the quest, and a symbol of the resumption of the 'natural' order to society. It would not be true to accuse Tolkien of giving his female characters no agency at all, though. In *The Silmarillion*, for example, Melian's ability to protect Doriath with her protection spell is strong enough to withstand the attempts of Ungoliant to pass through. Beren can only succeed in his quest for a Silmaril because he has the help of Lúthien. Shelob is no pet of Sauron, and Ungoliant, her even more fearsome progenitor, cannot be controlled even by Melkor, once the most powerful of the Ainur. Éowyn may choose to lay down her sword at the end but this does not make her weak, especially when one considers her strength of will throughout the text to this point. In other words, it would be far too simplistic to simply dismiss Tolkien as a misogynist; as ever, there is greater complexity at play here.

Issues regarding the depiction of female characters in Tolkien's work have been well-covered in the past by various critics, from Edwin Muir to Catherine Stimpson. There has also been some excellent scholarly work done on the question of gender in Tolkien's legendarium, and a great starting point is the essay 'The History of Scholarship on Female Characters in J.R.R. Tolkien's Legendarium: A Feminist Bibliographic Essay' by Robin Anne Reid, published in *Perilous and Fair: Women in the Life and Works of J.R.R. Tolkien*. Reid offers a detailed list of work in this area of study, starting in the 1970s where only two essays meet her criteria and on through to the 2000s in which, as she comments: "[d]uring the first decade of the twenty-first century, twenty-three articles and book chapters were published on Tolkien's female characters" – a significant increase (2015, 23). To help explain this, Reid looks to Dimitra Fimi who, in her monograph *Tolkien, Race and Cultural History: From Fairies to Hobbits*, observes that "Tolkien scholarship has started afresh during the last few years" and posits that one potential reason for the rise in academic interest in Tolkien's works is "the boundary between 'high' literature and fiction that appeals to mass audiences has become blurred, especially with the advent of 'theory' and cultural studies [...] In this context, Tolkien can be re-discovered and re-analysed in a serious way, a process that has already started in the last few years" (2010, 200-1). Whatever the reason, a fresh outlook on Tolkien's work can only be of benefit to the wider scholarly conversation.

Tolkien's portrayals of female characters were problematic, possibly because his views on gender were essentialist, as discussed by Anna Smol in her 'Gender in Tolkien's Works' entry in the *J.R.R. Tolkien Encyclopaedia*. Smol refers to Tolkien's 1941 letter to his son Michael in which he reveals his belief that part of women's "servient, helpmeet instinct" is "to be receptive, stimulated, fertilised (in many other matters than the physical) by the male" (*Letters*, Letter 43, 49). If, as Smol comments, this letter reveals that "Tolkien sees the male as naturally active and superior while the female is passive and subordinate by 'instinct'" (2007, 233), then we should probably not be surprised to find these beliefs resonating in his writing.

This paper does not seek to explore whether Tolkien was sexist, or a misogynist, or simply a man entrammelled in the opinions and beliefs of his time. Instead, the purpose of this paper is to examine specific concerns that relate to the issue of gender in Middle-earth, with particular reference to Dwarves: the absence of the maternal figure, the issue of procreation, and the lack of female presence within the narrative.

Female Dwarves, or Dwarf-women, do not feature greatly in the legendarium. The only female Dwarf who is named is Dís, the daughter of Thráin, and the mother of Fili and Kili, two Dwarves from *The Hobbit*, but she is mentioned only in Appendix A of *The Lord of the Rings* and not within the narrative itself. It is also discussed in Appendix A that, like the Elves and the Númenórean kings, the numbers of Dwarf-women are low, "probably no more than a third of the whole people" (*RK*, Appendix A, III). The main problem with the scarcity of Dwarf-women, of course, is that children may also be scarce. Tolkien refers directly to this predicament in 'The Later *Quenta Silmarillion*', in *The War of the Jewels*, when he writes: "It is said, also, that their womenkind are few, and that save their kings and chieftains few Dwarves ever wed; wherefore their race multiplied slowly and now is dwindling" (205). It is notable, therefore, that Tolkien himself acknowledged the scarcity of Dwarf-women and potential consequences of this.

The narrative does not indicate that Dwarves attached any great importance to the perpetuation of their race. In fact, Tolkien reveals the opposite to be true: not only do some Dwarf-women choose not to marry, but there also appears to be no sense of urgency regarding the situation amongst male Dwarves. In Appendix A, Tolkien tells us that "Thorin had no wife" (*RK*, Appendix A, III), thus illustrating the point that even the most important Dwarves rarely marry. Tolkien explains further:

It is because of the fewness of women amongst them that the kind of the Dwarves increases slowly, and is in peril when they have no secure dwellings. For Dwarves take only one wife or husband each in their lives [...] The number of Dwarf-men that marry is actually less than one-third. For not all the women take husbands: some desire none; some desire one that they cannot get, and so will have no other. As for the men, very many also do not desire marriage, being engrossed in their crafts. (III)

In *The Lord of the Rings* itself there is further evidence of a lack of attention towards reproduction among the Dwarves. Here, we encounter Gimli, the son of Glóin, who was one of the party of Dwarves in *The Hobbit*. There is never any reference to Gimli's mother, nor does Tolkien mention any siblings. There is no evidence within the narrative, the Appendix, nor even *The History of Middle-earth* series that Gimli ever marries or has children, possibly as a result of his great love for Galadriel and his reverence for her beauty, but also possibly due to the Dwarves' apparent absence of interest in procreation.

Dwarf-women are conspicuously missing from the legendarium. According to the 'Quenta Silmarillion' in *The Peoples of Middle-earth*, Aulë made only the *fathers* of the Dwarves and nowhere in the legendarium is there any record of the making of female Dwarves. Of Durin the Deathless, the eldest of these fathers of Dwarves, Tolkien observes that "his line never failed" (*Peoples*, 275), so he must have had children, but there is no mention of the Dwarf-women who must have been their mothers. It is interesting, however, that Tolkien had considered this question, seemingly at some length, whilst he was formulating his ideas on the making of the first Dwarves. According to Christopher Tolkien, his father had written a number of roughly drafted passages on this topic; it is in these notes, some of the most detailed of which are found in 'The Later *Quenta Silmarillion*' in the section 'Of the Naugrim and the Édain', that the only mention of the making of female Dwarves may be found. Here we can also track Tolkien's development of thought on the issue.

Note (a) indicates that Aulë made no Dwarf-women, but that Ilúvatar created them as mates for the males that Aulë had made:

(a) But it is said that to each Dwarf Ilúvatar added a mate of female kind, yet because he would not amend the work of Aulë, and Aulë had yet made only things of male form, therefore the women of the Dwarves resemble their men more than all other [?speaking] races. (*Jewels*, 203)

This is the only one of the notes that explains the existence of the Dwarf-women in this way – all the others show Aulë himself as creator of the females, although Tolkien offers several possible explanations for both their creation and their number. Both note (b) and note (c) show Aulë creating only six females to the seven males, with the reason given that he 'wearied' before he could make a seventh:

(b) He wrought in secret in a hall under the mountains in Middle-earth. There he made first one Dwarf, the eldest of all, and after he made six others, the fathers of their race; and then he began to make others again, like to them but of female kind to be their mates [...]

(c) Aulë made one, and then six, and he began to make mates for them of female form, and he made six, and then he wearied. Thus he buried six pairs, but one (Durin) the eldest he laid alone. (203)

It is interesting also that we are told in note (c) that Durin was laid alone. How, then, would his line continue? This is especially noteworthy as it is Durin who is singled out for the comment that his line never failed and not the other Dwarfs, for whom Aulë seemingly did create these unnamed, female mates.

In contrast, note (d) has Aulë creating an equal number of both, apparently in obedience to the desire of Ilúvatar:

(d) And Aulë took the Seven Dwarves and laid them to rest under stone on far-sundered places, and beside each [of] them he laid a mate as the Voice bade him, and then he returned to Valinor (author's parentheses). (203)

By note (e), however, Tolkien had reverted to his original idea of only six Dwarf-women to the seven Dwarf Fathers, with the eldest, Durin, being buried alone:

(e) Then Aulë took the Seven Dwarves and laid them to rest under stone in far-sundered places, and beside each he laid his mate, save only beside the Eldest, and he lay alone. And Aulë returned to Valinor and waited long as best he might. But it is not known when Durin or his brethren first awoke, though some think that it was at the time of the departure of the Eldar over sea. (203)

Why Tolkien decides this is not apparent from the text, but his decision again raises the conundrum of the continuation of Durin's line. This was not the end of Tolkien's musings on the issue, however. He continued this discussion in his Letter 212 to Rhona Beare in 1958, in which he reiterates the idea of there being seven Dwarf Fathers and six Dwarf-women, or 'mates', writing that Aulë "had made thirteen" and, in a note at the bottom of the page, confirming "One, the eldest, alone, and six more with six mates" (*Letters*, Letter 212, 287). Not for the first or, indeed, the last time, Tolkien appears to have been mulling over an issue in his writing that he fails to bring (for him, at least) to a satisfactory conclusion.

There are some important points to be made here. First, Tolkien's thoughts on the subject tended to an inequality in the numbers of Dwarf-women from the very beginning, thus presaging the difficulties the Dwarves would face in enabling the continuation of their species. Second, the Dwarf-women are specifically created as 'mates' for the Dwarf Fathers, with all the implications that come with such a term. Finally, and most significantly, despite all these draft passages and continued discussion in his letters, Tolkien discarded every one of these explanations for the existence of Dwarf-women and chose instead to excise them completely from the moment of creation. In his commentary on 'The Later *Quenta Silmarillion*', Christopher Tolkien notes: "In the final text, as printed in *The Silmarillion*, my father evidently abandoned the question of the origin of the female Dwarves, finding it intractable and the solutions unsatisfactory. Moreover, in the finished form the element of the Eldest (Durin) being distinct from the others, and without mate, finds no place" (*Jewels*, 212). Perhaps this issue, like the matter of the origin of the Orcs, proved troublesome enough for Tolkien that he never fully resolved it for himself. As a result, though, Dwarf-women are obscured even in their moment of origin.

From the very beginning of the histories of the Dwarves, then, it is clear that there is not only a lack of emphasis on reproduction, but also that Dwarf-women are seemingly invisible, their existence almost completely ignored. They appear to be of so little significance within Dwarf culture that they are removed from these Dwarf histories. In a note in 'The Making of Appendix A' on the absence of record concerning female Dwarves, Tolkien himself tells us that "They are seldom named in genealogies. They join their husbands' families. But if a son is seen to be 110 or so years younger than his father, this usually indicates an elder daughter. Thorin's sister Dís is named simply because of the gallant death of her sons Fili and Kili in defence of Thorin II" (*Peoples*, 285). This mention of a gap in the family tree indicating a female child is both significant and telling, as it is apparent that Dwarf-women have so little presence in Dwarf history that even the existence of daughters is excised from genealogies and records. Thus, apart from the few comments to be found within the Appendix to *The Lord of the Rings* and in *The History of Middle-earth* series, Tolkien omits Dwarf-women with no further explanation of their invisibility, and none are encountered in any of the narratives.

Dwarf-women, then, are present only in relation to the male Dwarves, a point that is emphasised by the way in which they are shaded from the eyes of the world. Tolkien describes in 'The Later *Quenta Silmarillion*' that female Dwarves are indiscernible from the males except in the fact that they rarely leave their homes to go out into the world, as "they go not to war and seldom save at direst need issue from their deep bowers and halls" (*Jewels*, 204). In her work *Desire in Language*, Julia Kristeva positions the figure of woman as "the silence or incoherence of the pre-discursive: she is the 'Other', which stands outside and threatens to disrupt the conscious (rational) order of speech" (1980, 132), which speaks to the situation of Tolkien's Dwarf-women. Although they are never, we are told, forced into marriage (*Peoples*, 285), nevertheless they live a life of seclusion, rarely entering the world and then never unaccompanied.

We may also note that their very femininity is disguised – even removed – as seen in the suggestion in Appendix A that they are so similar in appearance to the male Dwarves "that the eyes and ears of other people cannot tell them apart" (*RK*, Appendix A, III). According to the notes in 'The Later *Quenta Silmarillion*', Dwarf-women are also given the masculine indicator of beards and cannot "be discerned by those of other race, be it in feature or in gait or in voice" (*Jewels*, 205). Not even permitted their own physical form, female Dwarves are the 'invisible' women of Tolkien's legendarium; denied acknowledgement or recognition, they are situated on a border that separates Self and not-Self.

This does not mean, though, that they are entirely without agency. Tolkien tells us that Dwarf-women may choose not to marry and "are never forced to wed against their will" (*Peoples*, 285), thus implying that neither sex puts great emphasis on reproduction. As Dwarf-women have this choice, with marriage and childbearing not forced upon them, it becomes plain that they are not merely valued for the stereotypical gender role. Why, then, are they so hidden from view? Here, it might be useful to look to Simone de Beauvoir's thoughts on complicity. In *The Second Sex*, for example, de Beauvoir offers many examples of the ways in which women can be complicit in reinforcing what she refers to as "their own unfreedom" (2009, 667), due to socialisation, internalised misogyny and, importantly, the ways in which situation and coercive social setting can dictate complicity either through necessity, or through learned compliance. "Long-standing habit," she explains, can keep women's rights from "being correctly manifested" as society is inherently unequal and keeps women in an existential Otherness in which she is a passive object to man's active subject (9). As such, a woman "determines and differentiates herself in relation to man, and he does not in relation to her; she is the inessential in front of the essential. He is the subject, he is the absolute. She is the Other" (6). If we apply this thinking to Tolkien's Dwarf-women, it is clear that there is a question to be asked about their position within their own culture, especially in terms of identity.

With the similarity in appearance to male Dwarves, and the lack of emphasis on the traditionally female role of 'mother', how do Dwarf-women identify themselves? Kimberly Carter-Cram, in a discussion of de Beauvoir's ideas on positions of Self, defines identity as pertaining to "one's individuality, indeed to the lack of 'sameness' of one's character, as these traits express themselves in a variety of different times and situations" (1997, 86). However, the only identity that the Dwarf-women have that is accessible by the reader is constructed for them solely through Tolkien's notes in Appendix A, and *The History of Middle-earth* series. It is significant that these notes, like the Dwarf-women, stand outside the narrative.

In *The Second Sex*, de Beauvoir discusses such loss of identity and refers to it as the 'feminine lack', the negative space against which the masculine identity differentiates itself (2009, xvii). In appearance, male and female Dwarves are so similar that this is not offered as a way to distinguish between them. Instead, the reader may recognise the figure of the male Dwarf by, for example, the fact that he goes out into the world – in other words, one gender may be determined by what the other is not. Jenny Robinson follows Judith Butler's theories on this point, when she makes the argument that 'gender identities' are "produced in the performative (re)-iteration of culturally specific understandings of masculinity and femininity" (2000, 289). In her essay 'Sex and Gender in Simone de Beauvoir's Second Sex', Butler understands de

Beauvoir's famous assertion that "one is not born, but rather becomes a woman" as enabling a differentiation between the terms 'sex' and 'gender' (de Beauvoir 2009, 301). Butler reads this as suggesting that 'gender' is an aspect of identity that is "gradually acquired", pointing towards a more radical understanding of gender (1986, 35). If this is the case, one must question how the Dwarf-women are able to identify as female, as so little seems to be offered to them to enable the formulation of such an understanding of gender.

The only identity accessible to Tolkien's Dwarf-women, therefore, is constructed through simple biology: they are female and may bear children. This forces them to be read as having one common identity, a problem that Butler highlights in her essay 'Gender Trouble.' "If one 'is' a woman," she declares:

> that surely is not all one is; the term fails to be exhaustive, not because a pre-gendered 'person' transcends the specific paraphernalia of its gender, but because gender is not always constituted coherently or consistently in different historical contexts, and because gender intersects with racial, class, ethnic, sexual, and regional modalities of discursively constituted identities." (31)

Reducing the identity of Dwarf-women to gender denies them any other characteristics that may offer individuality, rather than a collective signifier. Within Tolkien's legendarium, there are no female Dwarf characters that might enable the reader to formulate an impression of personality, disposition, behaviour, or features. If, as Anoop Nayak and Mary Jane Kehily contend, "identity is a type of 'doing' that is only made manifest at the point of action", then this is something to which Dwarf-women can have little claim (2006, 459). As Butler asserts, "[t]he limits to gender, the range of possibilities for a lived interpretation of a sexually differentiated anatomy, seem less restricted by anatomy itself than by the weight of the cultural institutions which have conventionally interpreted anatomy" (1986, 45). It is not merely biology that restricts Tolkien's Dwarf-women; their location within Dwarf culture, and the resulting interpretations of Dwarf gender norms, is the most limiting factor.

The figure of the Dwarf-woman, silenced through lack of representation in the narrative and hidden by means of (author-enforced) physical disguise, therefore suffers almost total loss of identity in the Middle-earth legendarium. With no sense of Self except in relation to the male Dwarves, she cannot say "I am here", only "He is here, I am elsewhere." She is not merely marginalised; she is also effectively excluded from the narrative. The Dwarf-woman is the most contained of all the females in Middle-earth, made 'Other' by her own race. If gender differences are socially or culturally constructed, and that culture places constraints on one gender's ability to create individual identities, then this may go some way to explain the invisibility of the Dwarf-women of Middle-earth.

Bibliography

de Beauvoir, Simone, *The Second Sex* (1949), trans. Borde, C. & Malovany-Chevallier, S. (New York: Random House 2009).

Butler, Judith, 'Sex and Gender in Simone de Beauvoir's Second Sex', in *Yale French Studies* 72 (1986), 35-49.
--- 'Gender Trouble', in *Continental Feminism Reader*, ed. by Cahill, A. J. & Hansen, J. (Maryland: Rowman & Littlefield, 2003) pp. 29-56.

Carter-Cram, Kimberley, 'Identity Crises: Positions of Self in Simone de Beauvoir's Memoires', in *Paroles Gelées: UCLA French Studies* Special Issue, 15.2 (1997), 83-93.

Fimi, Dimitra, *Tolkien, Race and Cultural History: From Fairies to Hobbits*, (London: Palgrave Macmillan, 2010).

Kristeva, Julia, *Desire in Language: A Semiotic Approach to Literature and Art*, ed. by Leon S. Roudiez (New York, Columbia University Press, 1980).

Nayak, Anoop, & Kehily, Mary Jane, 'Gender Undone: Subversion, Regulation and Embodiment in the Work of Judith Butler', in *British Journal of Sociology of Education*, 27.4 (2006), 459-472.

Reid, Robin Anne, 'The History of Scholarship on Female Characters in J.R.R. Tolkien's Legendarium: A Feminist Bibliographic Essay', in *Perilous and Fair: Women in the Life and Works of J.R.R. Tolkien*, ed. by Janet Brennan Croft and Leslie A. Donovan (Altadena, Ca: Mythopoeic Press, 2015), pp.13-40.

Robinson, Jenny. 'Feminism and the Spaces of Transformation' in *Transactions of the Institute of British Geographers* New Series, 25.3 (2000), 285-330.

Smol, Anna, 'Gender in Tolkien's Works', in *J.R.R. Tolkien Encyclopaedia: Scholarship and Critical Assessment*, ed. by Michael D.C. Drout (New York: Routledge, 2007), pp. 233-235.

Tolkien, J.R.R., *The Letters of J.R.R. Tolkien*, ed. by Humphrey Carpenter with the assistance of Christopher Tolkien (London: Harper Collins, 1981).
--- *The War of the Jewels*, ed. by Christopher Tolkien (London: HarperCollins, 1994)
--- *The Lord of the Rings*, (London: Harper Collins, 1995).
--- *The Peoples of Middle-earth*, ed. by Christopher Tolkien (London: HarperCollins, 1996).

The Lossoth: Indigeneity, Representation, and Antiracism

Nicholas Birns[1]

In Appendix A of *The Lord of the Rings*, we are told that Arvedui, the last king of the line of Valandil in the North, takes refuge from the Witch-King in the collapse of his own kingdom of Arthedain in Third Age 1974, with the Lossoth. The Lossoth, described as "the Snowmen of Forochel" are Northern, polar-area Indigenous people clearly modelled on the Inuit, Sámi, or Nenets (*RK*, Appendix A, I, iii). Tolkien says of the Lossoth: "They built their homes from snow and, in sliding carts and skates of bone, they crossed the ice lands and hunted the thick-furred animals from which they fashioned their clothes" (iii). Robert Foster, in his *Guide to Middle-earth*, describes the Lossoth as "primitive and poor" (1978, 305). The Lossoth take in Arvedui and his men after their defeat by the Witch-King of Angmar. They do this partly out of "pity" and partly out of "fear" (*RK*, Appendix A, I, iii).

Arvedui lives for a short time in harmony and mutual assistance with the Lossoth. He even gives the heirloom of his house, the Ring of Barahir, to these Indigenous people, recognizing that they are kin enough to receive this ancient symbol of the Edain. Arvedui is able to at least temporarily recognize that people not phenotypically white can, in Eliza Farrell's words, "contribute their own worth" (2009, 37).

1. Especially since this paper deals with fantasy representations of Indigenous people, I would like to acknowledge the Lenape, the traditional owners of the land where I live now.

The Lossoth know and feel situated in their own physical environment in a way Arvedui does not, but he has the wisdom to "seek help" from them (iii). This saves the king's life. Arvedui, though, does not heed the advice of the Lossoth not to board the ship that will take him back South. The unnamed chief of the Lossoth says to Arvedui: "Do not mount on this sea-monster! If they have them, let the seamen bring us food and other things that we need, and you may stay here till the Witch-King goes home. For in summer his power wanes; but now his breath is deadly, and his cold arm is long" (iii). But Arvedui, thinking he knows better, does not listen. He dies in a shipwreck in Third Age 1975. Arvedui's poignant story is ultimately mobilized into the genealogy of Aragorn's kingship and Númenórean restoration. This mobilization parallels how the indigeneity of the Lossoth is reinscribed into an avatar of colonialism rather than valued for itself.

The story of the Lossoth reveals the tantalizing potential of diversity in Tolkien's represented world and a corollary tendency for conventional valuations of whiteness and hierarchy to obdurately reassert themselves. Yet, as in the cognate role played by the people of Ghân-buri-Ghân in the War of the Ring, the momentary appearance of the Lossoth is still meaningful. This is particularly so as they are geographically positioned at the extreme north and west of Middle-earth, the two compass-points that Tolkien elsewhere values as an analogue for his own Europe. I contend that the Lossoth intermittently operate as an internal brake upon Eurocentrism, and an indicator that resistance to evil cannot be channelled through one model of identity or belonging.

Tolkien takes the Lossoth out of what might be called an axiological binary, a dyad of value, as they are clearly not evil. Indeed, the Lossoth do their best to help Arvedui. The limits of the help they can give him are also, as in a mirror, the limits of the Arthedain leader's cultural sensitivity. But the Lossoth are still in an anthropological binary. They are seen as, despite having their own intuitive wisdom, less noble and consequential than Arvedui and his kind.

What did Tolkien actually know about northern Indigenous people? John Garth sees the aid to Arvedui and his men of the "wary Lossoth" as reminiscent of the interaction of the Arctic Inuit with Sir John Franklin and the men of his expedition who perished in the 1850s (2020, 70). There were many European ethnographies of the Inuit that would have been available to Tolkien in his youth. Of these, some were frankly racialised, not just in terms of seeing the Inuit as lower and primitive but in denying them their very identity. In John Steckley's *White Lies About the Inuit* (2008), it is revealed that Victorian and Edwardian narratives in the UK and Canada loved to speculate about blonde Inuit populations, often described as survivors of medieval Viking shipwrecks. Thus in *Boy Scouts of the North* (1920), an Inuit named Saanak is described as "different from [...] the rest of his tribe" (quoted in Steckley 2008, 90). Saanak has blue eyes and "hair and beard of a golden red" (90). Similarly, in *The Aryan Māori* (1885) Edward Tregear tried to whiten the Indigenous people of Aotearoa (New Zealand). Tolkien preferred racialised representation of northern Indigenous people. But at least he respected some measure of cultural integrity.

Contemporary representations of Indigenous people were not Tolkien's only conceivable source for the Lossoth. Adam Miyashiro, in a pivotal intervention, has analyzed the character of Grendel in *Beowulf* as a "proto-indigenous" figure (2020, 384). In Miyashiro's analysis, Grendel unsettles Danish political and social authority. Building on Miyashiro's contention that the idea of Indigeneity is pertinent to the world of *Beowulf*, I would add that the poet, if he operated at the very latest date scholars have postulated, was near to having possible knowledge of North American Indigenous people via the Viking voyages. This knowledge would require an early eleventh-century date for the poem, i. e. after the Norse voyages to Greenland and Vinland, and the encounter with the Indigenous 'Skraelings', usually viewed as either Inuit or Beothuk (see Weaver 2014, 36). Indeed, the Cherokee scholar and writer Jace Weaver posited the year 1000 as the inception-point of the 'Red Atlantic', a cultural space of trans-Indigeneity which encompasses "the Atlantic and its major adjacent bodies of water" (2014, 15).

Even if one accepts an earlier, pre-Greenland and Vinland date for the poem, there is a possibility of actual Indigenous referents in *Beowulf*. Readers of *Beowulf* will remember the episode in which Unferth, the (as Tolkien calls him in Sellic Spell) 'Unfriend' at the court of Hrothgar, taunts Beowulf with the knowledge of his brash swimming-duel with Breca (*Beowulf*, 382). In this duel, Beowulf is alleged to have conducted himself with unheroic showboating. Beowulf ripostes that he showed supreme bravery and stamina in this episode, slaying multiple sea beasts and swimming all the way to the coast of "Finna-land" (Arnold 1876, 42). It is tempting to read this as denoting, in ethnographic terms, the land dwelled in by the present-day Finns, the people of the *Kalevala* and Jean Sibelius, the Finno-Ugric speaking Suomi. Yet the Roman historian Tacitus, when he spoke of the *Fenni*, is said by the nineteenth-century scholar Lars Levi Laestadius (himself part-Indigenous) to have been speaking of the Sámi, the Indigenous people who were called Lapps by others, when he spoke of the *Fenni*. Tacitus's Finns, and thereby the Finns known to the early Germanic peoples, may well have not been Suomi, the people known today as Finns, but Sámi (see also Valtonen 2008, 75). As Astri Dankertsen points out, the Sámi share a history of victimization by "racialization and scientific racism" with "other indigenous peoples" (2019, 110). R.W. Chambers, whose work Tolkien cited in his "Monsters and the Critics" essay, spoke of Sámi cultural contact with the cultural "traces" of the peoples described in *Beowulf* (1921, 249). The Scride-Finns of the early English poem *Widsith*, were similarly taken to be "undoubtedly" Sámi by Columbian professor Elliott V. K. Dobbie in the 1950s – who was a traditional philologist in his methodology, like Chambers (1953, xliv).

In other words, there is a possibility of an Arctic indigeneity referred to on the periphery of the *Beowulf* poem itself. Tolkien's invention of the Lossoth as a Northern Indigenous people on the periphery of the Edain of western Middle-earth was, to use the term popularized by Tom Shippey, a "calque" (1982, 66). But it was a calque not just of the world Tolkien knew. It was also because of the Sámi-Beowulf connection that a calque of the world of his philological research. This is not to say the Lossoth were not inspired by North American Indigenous peoples: the Inuit, who after all had close contact with speakers of the languages Tolkien studied in Greenland, or the Beothuk that the Vikings most likely briefly encountered in Newfoundland. But the idea of Northern Indigenous peoples sharing continental space with people phenotypically white existed both in medieval Europe and in the represented world of Tolkien's Third Age Middle-earth. Tolkien's medieval scholarship such as his "Sigelwara-land" essay has led Brian McFadden and Margaret Sinex to conclude that it included a somewhat problematic acknowledgment of Black African peoples to the south of the world Tolkien privileged geographically. Similarly, the implied world-view of Tolkien's fictionalised legendarium can somewhat grudgingly include non-white, Indigenous people to the North, like the Sámi.

Dimitra Fimi notes that the Drúedain, revealed in *Unfinished Tales* as the people of Ghân-buri-Ghân, are given "child-like characteristics" (2009, 150). Fimi further notes that the racial taxonomy of the era into which Tolkien was born stereotyped Indigenous people as more "automatic" and "instinctive" (150). Arvedui accepts the help of the Lossoth; he trusts the Snowmen with his most cherished possessions. He even for a time genuinely listens to their advice. Yet Arvedui continuously maintains his own sense of privilege and social status; he holds himself aloof from the Lossoth such as the Dúnedain often saw themselves as "a superior race that stood apart from all the others" (Fimi 2009, 148). Arvedui's heedless self-confidence is an example of "invisible whiteness" which Robin Anne Reid characterizes as haunting latter-day medievalism, including Tolkien and Tolkien Studies (2017, 36).

Appendix A to *The Lord of the Rings* is replete with signifiers of race, ethnicity, and identity. This is particularly true of those aspects of the third and fourth sections of the Appendix (centering on Arnor and Gondor respectively) which are set in the twentieth and twenty-first centuries—of Third Age Middle-earth. I contend (bolstered by Tolkien's use of near future dates in *The Notion Club Papers*) that Tolkien was semi-intentionally putting the fall of Arthedain in a twentieth century (if not *our* twentieth century), in what was for Tolkien, writing in the 1940s, the near-future date of 1975. In this, Tolkien was making an oblique point that he was considering issues germane to his own times. Tolkien sets up a contrast between Arvedui, who is willing to listen to Indigenous people like the Lossoth, and Eärnur, who listens to no one – even an Elf of renown such as Glorfindel. This prepares for a genealogy characterized by (to adapt Bernard Williams's phrase) moral luck where Eärnur dies childless but Arvedui's multiplied great-grandson Aragorn gets to ascend the throne of both Gondor and Arnor. But we must remember that Arvedui listened incompletely. His failure to heed the Lossoth's caution about the ship led to his premature doom.

Tolkien's representation of the Lossoth gives visibility to non-Europeans in a manner corollary to the actual situation of medieval Europe which did have contact with Indigenous peoples in Greenland, Vinland, and the lands of the Sámi. This forestalls the erasure of Indigenous peoples which would result from their not being represented at all. Tolkien certainly avoids the extremes of European racist representation. But the representation of the Lossoth is still encased in what Fimi has called a "hierarchical world" (2009, 141). They remain marginal to the main action and personages of the text. As Tolkien himself apologetically admitted in letter 151 to Naomi Mitchison, the ice-bay of Forochel was not "cast for any significant part" in the book, even though he had presumably by this time envisioned its role in Arvedui's end (*Letters*, 212).

Moreover, there is an extra twist in the plot here. As Jes Battis has pointed out, the Hobbits themselves are "socially marginalized" and "culturally othered" (2004, 949). This racialization coincides with (to use James Buzard's term) an autoethnographic authorial move to see the Hobbits as like his posited readers (2005). Thus there is a self-racialization which precludes genuine alterity. This lack can be seen in two very specific details by which the Hobbits and Lossoth are paralleled. Firstly, they both fear ships and the sea. This fear both indicates that they understand the association with death the sea has in Tolkien but also are shy of the Valinor-drawn enlightenment that those beings who assay the sea successfully possess. Secondly, both the Hobbits and the Lossoth try to aid King Arvedui. Indeed, in narrative terms, the first thing we hear about Arvedui in the Prologue, is the support a band of Hobbit bowmen give him in the last battle against the Witch-King. Both Hobbits and Lossoth, in other words, try to aid the nonetheless doomed Arvedui. They survive beneath the King's folly, even though both lack his grandeur. Indeed, whereas presumably the lore about the Lossoth in Appendix A is from the records of Gondor, the tale of the Hobbit bowmen who aided Arvedui is recorded in "no tales of Men" (*FR*, 'Prologue', 5). This relativizes away the genuine, albeit limited, difference Tolkien achieved in the depiction of the Lossoth. Here, the Lossoth are likened to a people fundamentally depicted as shorter, furrier versions of white Europeans.

There are residues of this sort of depiction when we consider the probable genealogy of the Lossoth within Tolkien's oeuvre. A possible early trace of the Lossoth is to be found in *Letters from Father Christmas* as the "Snowboys, sons of the Snowmen, which are the only sorts of people that live near – not of course men made of snow" (56). The Snowboys stem far more from a Santa Claus mythology than any anthropologically rich representation of Northern peoples. But they are said to be not *made of snow*, but *living in the far North in the snow*. The snow-context puts them in the place of people such as the Inuit as a kind of substitute. This choice is disturbing in several ways. It replaces the actual people of the area with a white-dominated mythology and the demographic reality with fairy-tale stereotypes, while further relinquishing and distorting the great asset and historicity of the legends Tolkien studied in his professional work. Lossoth certainly sounds more dignified than Snowboys, just as '*Periannath*'

NICHOLAS BIRNS

sounds less cutesy or cuddly than 'Hobbits.' Yet no amount of Sindarinisation can gentrify away the sense that the actual Indigenous peoples (represented by the Lossoth) are shadowed by the residue of the Santa-ambient Snowboys. Or one could say that the Lossoth are a halfway point between the emptiness of the far northern Helcaraxë in *The Silmarillion* and the cozy Santa-mythology of the *Father Christmas* letters. Tolkien was a genius at repurposing and redefining elements in his personal mythology so as to deepen them. We see him doing this in *The Lord of the Rings* not only with the Hobbits but the character of Tom Bombadil. Bombadil, notably, was called an "Aborigine" (*Shadow*, 117) in early drafts of *The Lord of the Rings*, this word denoting that he was there before anyone else. Tolkien wisely did not use this word in the final draft. Instead, he cast the Lossoth and the Druédain as Indigenous peoples who were not phenotypically white in the same way that Bombadil was.

Moreover, the link to the *Father Christmas* letters connects the Lossoth to a milieu (albeit in a fantastic vein) set unquestionably in the twentieth century. Tolkien dated the letters with contemporary dates, feigning that Father Christmas was writing to his children in 1920, 1923, and so on. This reinforces the way that the Hobbits and Lossoth both emerge into history by aiding Arvedui in the twentieth century (Third Age), suggesting that the depictions of both peoples were also about Tolkien's *now*. In other words, that Indigenous peoples were still there. They had shown fortitude and what the Anishinabe writer Gerald Vizenor termed "survivance," which he defines as "an active sense of presence over absence" (2008, 1). Thus they outlined Eurocentric imperialism.

Rendering non-white people as visible in the sphere of whiteness without extreme or visible racism, as Tolkien did in representing the Lossoth, is an achievement. Is that enough?

Not at all. Tolkien had no interest in the Lossoth other than in this particular scene. The representation of the Lossoth still is inhabited by condescension and white privilege. Ibram X. Kendi has contended that racist postures are "detached" from ascribed identity (2019, 200). Thus there are no racist or antiracist people, that "we can be a racist one minute and antiracist the next" (10). Therefore it might be plausible to say that it is the racism or antiracism inherent in the act of reading which is more relevant for us, than the racism or antiracism of the texts themselves. Texts, though, are not people. The most antiracist reading cannot make a racist text antiracist. But it can arguably problematize the racism within that text.

The presence of the Lossoth in the Third Age of Middle-earth extends even further the "cultural exchange" that Sandra R. Straubhaar sees exemplified in the mixed marriages of the Gondorian kings and the northern wild men of Rhovanion (2001, 116). But it makes Straubhaar's conclusion that Tolkien does not "celebrate racism" problematic (116). The second millennium of Third Age Middle-earth as chronicled in Appendix A is replete with racial signifiers, particularly the paradox that Angamaitë and Sangahyando (the leaders of the Corsairs of Umbar whose Haradrim descendants are present in *The Return of the King*) are among the most racialized figures in the novel as they are described as pure-blooded men of the West. This was a point Tolkien reiterated in one of his last letters, Letter 347, to Richard Jeffery, where Tolkien said that the Númenórean descent to the rebel leaders was "clear" (*Letters*, 371). Pure Númenórean blood does not guarantee virtue, and those of part-Rhovanion ancestry can still be virtuous Gondorian kings. But clearly the white wild people of Rhovanion have access to a greater macro-history of Middle-earth that the non-white Indigenous Lossoth do not. This is true even though both peoples are clearly a manifestation of Tolkien's desire to render a wide cultural tableau.

Nothing in Tolkien fully speaks to the condition of Indigenous people or helps those people be heard. For some Tolkien fans in Aotearoa (New Zealand) who saw Peter Jackson's *The Fellowship of the Ring* upon its release in 2001, the most poignant moment for them might have been the Māori words in the credits. This multilingualism coexisted with the film's multilingual parading of Tolkien's invented languages in ways that juxtaposed but obviously, as Sue Kim's work reminds us, did not parallel or coincide performances of difference (2004, 880). Similarly, representations of racialized others in Middle-earth remind us of reality but do not approach it. Even as we continue to enjoy and critique Tolkien, we should also read outstanding Indigenous writers writing in North America, Oceania, and elsewhere. These writers have contributed and are still emerging worldwide and heed the ongoing calls for justice for Indigenous people. What Reid calls the "growing awareness of racism as [...] systematic and institutional" should not exculpate Tolkien's texts from responsibility for the failures of their racial representations (2017, 54). But this awareness does allow for acts of reading, hopefully ever more scrupulous and granular and culturally attuned, that will perhaps allow us to listen more attentively than Arvedui did in 1975 of the Third Age.

Bibliography

Arnold, Thomas, *Beowulf: A Heroic Poem of the Eighth Century*, (London: Longman. 1876).

Battis, Jes, 'Gazing Upon Sauron: Hobbits, Elves, and the Queering of the Postcolonial Optic,' *Modern Fiction Studies*, 50:4 (2004): 949–979.

Buzard, James, *Disorienting Fictions: The Autoethnographic Work of Nineteenth-Century English Novels*, (Princeton: Princeton University Press, 2005).

Chambers, R. W., *Beowulf: An Introduction*, (Cambridge: Cambridge University Press, 1921).

Dankertsen, Astri, 'I Felt So White: Sámi Racialization, Indigeneity, and Shades of Whiteness,' *Native American and Indigenous Studies*, 6:2 (2019), 110–137.

Dobbie, Elliott Van Kirk, *Beowulf and Judith*, (New York: Columbia University Press, 1953).

Farrell, Eliza, 'Race, Language, and Morality: Does Tolkien's Middle-earth promote a Racial Myth,' unpublished thesis, University of Pittsburgh, 2009.

Fimi, Dimitra, *Tolkien, Race and Cultural History: From Fairies to Hobbits*, (Basingstoke: Palgrave Macmillan, 2009).

Foster, Robert W., *The Complete Guide to Middle-earth: From The Hobbit to the Silmarillion*, (New York: Ballantine, 1978).

Garth, John, *The Worlds of J.R.R. Tolkien*, (Princeton: Princeton University Press, 2020).

Kendi, Ibram X, *How To be An Antiracist*, (New York: One World, 2019).

Kim, Sue, 'Beyond Black and White: Race and Postmodernism in *The Lord of the Rings* Film,' *Modern Fiction Studies*, 50: 4 (2004): 875–907.

McFadden, Brian, 'Fear of Difference, Fear of Death: The Sigelwara, Tolkien's Swertings, and Racial Difference', in *Tolkien's Modern Middle Ages*, ed. by Jane Chance and A.K. Siewers (Basingstoke: Palgrave Macmillan, 2009) pp. 155-169.

Miyashiro, Adam, 'Homeland Insecurity: Biopolitics and Sovereign Violence in *Beowulf*,' *Postmedieval*, 11 (2020), 384-95.

Reid, R.A., 'Race in Tolkien Studies: A Bibliographic Essay,' in *Tolkien and Alterity*, ed. by Christopher Vaccaro and Yvonne Kisor, (New York: Palgrave Macmillan, 2017), pp. 33-76.

Shippey, T. A., *The Road to Middle-earth*, (London: Allen and Unwin, 1982).

Sinex, Margare,. '"Monsterized Saracens", Tolkien's Haradrim, and Other Medieval "Fantasy Products"', *Tolkien Studies*, 7.7 (2010), 175-196.

Straubhaar, Sandra R., 'Myth, Late Roman History, and Multiculturalism in Tolkien's Middle-earth,' in *Tolkien and the Invention of Myth: A Reader*, ed. Jane Chance, (Lexington: University Press of Kentucky, 2004), pp. 101–117.

Steckley, John, *White Lies About The Inuit*, (Toronto: University of Toronto Press, 2008).

Tolkien, J.R.R., *The Fellowship of the Ring*, (Boston: Houghton Mifflin, 1976).
--- *The Return of the King* (Boston: Houghton Mifflin, 1976).
--- *Letters from Father Christmas*, ed. Baillie Tolkien (New York: Houghton Mifflin, 1976).
--- *The Letters of J. R. R. Tolkien*, ed. Humphrey Carpenter with the assistance of Christopher Tolkien, (Boston: Houghton Mifflin, 1981).
--- *The Return of the Shadow*, (Boston: Houghton Mifflin, 1988).
--- *Sauron Defeated: The End of the Third Age* (New York: Harper Collins, 1992).
--- *Beowulf, A Translation and Commentary, Together With Sellic Spell* (New York: Houghton Mifflin Harcourt, 2014).

Tregear, Edward, *The Aryan Maori*, (Wellington: Didsbury, 1885).

Valtonen, Iremeli, *The North In The Old English Orosius*, (Helsinki: Sociéte Neophilologique, 2008).

Vizenor, Gerald, *Survivance: Narratives of Native Presence*, (Lincoln: University of Nebraska Press, 2008).

Weaver, Jace, *The Red Atlantic: American Indigenes and the Making of the Modern World* (Chapel Hill: University of North Carolina Press, 2014).

Williams, Bernard, *Moral Luck: Philosophical Papers, 1973-1980*, (Cambridge: Cambridge University Press, 1981).

"The Burnt Hand Teaches Most About Fire": Applying Trauma Exposure and Ecological Frameworks to Narratives of Displacement and Resettlement Across Elven Cultures in Tolkien's Middle-earth

V. Elizabeth King

J.R.R. Tolkien created a world brimming with diverse peoples, races, and cultures, their development as inherently complex as the intricate histories and plots that underlie them.[1] There is no racial, ethnic, or cultural group untouched by the events set into motion by Melkor's original discontent, which rippled across Arda in numerous forms, two effects being trauma and displacement. Refugee and migration narratives are key themes in Tolkien's legendarium, with nearly everyone in Middle-earth experiencing some type of forced displacement, which, in the "real world", is highly correlated with both trauma exposure and traumatic stress. Because these are concepts that Tolkien represents both explicitly and implicitly in his legendarium and personal histories, it is reasonable to apply them to his works.

1. I would like to thank the numerous kind and brilliant members of the Silmarillion Writers' Guild who not only supported and inspired me as I worked on this project but also tolerated my – not insignificant – anxiety. Special SWG thanks to Dawn Wells-Thumma, Gaia Lambruschi, and Bunn. Finally, thanks to Kirsty Malone (fan-friend and unexpected mentor) and to Hannah Mendro (fan-friend and graduate student in Cultural Studies at the University of Washington) for providing a second set of eyes on early drafts.

Just as in refugee and trauma literature, memory dominates the narratives of Tolkien's myths, as well as his personal and professional orientations. In a 1958 letter to Rhona Beare, he eschewed a purely theological interpretation of his works by stating they were "concerned with Death, and Immortality; and the 'escapes': serial longevity, and hoarding memory" (Letter 211, 284). In contrast to the issue of hoarded memory in the legendarium, in a letter to his son Christopher during World War II, Tolkien writes: "The utter stupid waste of war, not only material but moral and spiritual, is so staggering to those who have to endure it. [...] But so short is human memory and so evanescent are its generations that in only about 30 years there will be few or no people with that direct experience which alone goes really to the heart. The burnt hand teaches most about fire" (Letter 64, 76). This balance of memory – the context of one's experiences and the time and place in which one's memories are made – and its useful application seems to have been important to Tolkien.

This paper will therefore combine trauma and social ecological frameworks to illuminate the ways in which textual evidence of trauma and migration may have affected cultural development in the three largest, remaining elven realms in Middle-earth at the end of the Third Age (T.A.). By mapping modern conceptions of trauma and displacement onto Elrond (Imladris); Amroth and Galadriel (Lothlórien); and Oropher and Thranduil (Mirkwood), this paper will define ways in which individual and group-level experiences may have affected these leaders' life outcomes, influencing the settings they created and the cultures in which they immersed themselves. At a time in our world in which displacement is occurring at one of the highest rates in recorded history, such an application may remind us of the continued relevance of Tolkien's work.

1 - Theoretical Orientation

Social ecological models help researchers understand the individual in context (Lounsbury and Mitchell 2009, 214). The model situates the individual at the center of a system containing family, community, institutions, society/culture, and time/history in concentric and interacting circles. While individuals possess their own innate psychological or genetic inclinations, the expression of those traits, their development, and experiences are affected also by the levels around them: a child is impacted by their family, a family by their culture, etc. However, the actions of the individual also bidirectionally influence the social ecological levels around *them*: nothing, therefore, is strictly independent. Timing and history are also important parts of the model: an individual will be differentially impacted by events and their environment depending on what time in life they are occurring. Time is also important at higher ecological levels. For example, a parent's past experiences may impact behavior in the family unit. Societally, a history of conflict in the region may have a lasting impact on all other levels, including influences on individual belief and behavior. In short, actions and choices are not only internal to individual beliefs and cognition but are also embedded in situation, context, and environment.

In psychological and clinical contexts, trauma is generally defined as "the experience [...] of events that are life-threatening or include a danger of injury so severe that a person is horrified, feels helpless, and experiences a psychophysiological alarm response" (Schauer, Neuner, and Elbert 2005, 7). In addition to direct threat to self, being surrounded by violence in a war zone or seeing dead bodies are considered traumatic events (International Society for Traumatic Stress Studies 2021). Post-traumatic stress disorder and related disorders are characterized by re-experiencing the event, avoiding reminders of the event, experiencing negative changes to behavior and cognition, and hyperarousal and reactivity; complex PTSD may involve an inability to trust others and poor self-image (ISTSS 2021). Trauma exposure is also associated with anxiety and depression. Trauma and mental health generally function in a dose-effect response, meaning that the severity of symptoms correlates with the duration and number of traumatic events (Masten and Narayan 2012, 230).

Trauma exposure in Tolkien's world has varied effects, something psychopathology calls "multifinality," i.e., people may have similar experiences but end up with different outcomes (Luthar, Cicchetti, and Becker 2000, 555).[2] For example, in contrast to pathological outcomes, trauma exposure can also be associated with resilience and post-traumatic growth. This might manifest as being better able to handle daily stress; being more likely to experience empathy; and being more likely than their peers without trauma to demonstrate compassion through service (Patel et al. 2017, 121; Greenberg et al. 2018, 6; Vollhardt and Staub 2011, 312). Emerging research suggests that people with a trauma history are more likely to volunteer with disadvantaged groups, and that a shared trauma type (e.g., natural disaster) increases prosocial behavior (Vollhardt and Staub 2011, 313).

Finally, intergenerational transmission of trauma is well-supported. It may be passed on through a number of

2. And given Tolkien's own experiences with trauma exposure, this realistic reflection is unsurprising.

mechanisms, like genetics, parenting behaviors, caregiver mental health, and risk environments (Isobel et al. 2018, 1107; Morelli et al. 2020, 172; Bryant et al. 2018, 256; Cobham and Newnham 2020, 160). This intergenerational influence is highlighted in Tolkien's writing, with the Oath of Fëanor and the Children of Húrin being prime examples. While Tolkien explicitly rejects trauma-related struggle and traumatic stress as a "moral failure", he nevertheless consistently positions the most noble response to trauma as one that turns the suffering of the self toward the service of others (*Letters*, Letter 246, 326). Elrond is the best example of Tolkien's conceptualization of the ideal and noble response to traumatic events. Throughout the legendarium, Elrond is transformed from refugee to orphan to lord to humanitarian as an unintended result of his life experiences.

2 - "Kind as Summer": Elrond and Transformative Trauma

Defining what Elrond *is*, culturally, is a challenge. His parentage tells us he could be considered Noldorin, Maiarin, Vanyarin, Sindarin, and Man. Elrond and Elros were born in the Havens of Sirion among Sindarin and Noldorin refugees from both Gondolin and Doriath. Later, they were fostered for a time by Maglor.[3] Elrond and Elros's pedigree and cultural positioning have significance because of the emphasis placed on lineage and hierarchy in the legendarium. While they have the blood of the three Elven clans, the three houses of the mannish Edain, and the Ainur, they also have extended periods

---

3. What all this means is that we can say that Elrond had significant early influence from his parents; from whomever the other survivors of Doriath and Gondolin were at Sirion, including some groups of Men; and then also, at least briefly, from the sons of Fëanor and their folk.

of contact with ethnicities outside of their family. Such an ethnically complex backstory lends itself to a family history marked by the violence and migrations endemic to life in Middle-earth: their paternal and maternal lines reveal a history of constant trauma exposure and displacement. To highlight the ways in which trauma experienced by one family member interacts with others intergenerationally – and thus emphasize the degree to which Elrond and Elros are potentially affected by their social ecological contexts – a detailed family trauma history is included in the Appendix with a family tree.

2.1 - Elrond and Elros's Early Life and Elrond's Trauma-related History

Elrond and Elros were born at the Mouths of Sirion in the First Age (F.A.) 532. The Third Kinslaying occurred in F.A. 538, when they were six years old. Eärendil was away and Elwing fled with the Silmaril. The majority of the refugees living in and around Sirion were killed, as well as a number of dissenting Feanorians. Elrond and Elros were taken in by one of the remaining sons of Fëanor, for "Maglor took pity upon [the children], and he cherished them, and love grew after between them" (*Silmarillion*, 306). How long they spent with Maglor is unclear, but by F.A. 587, Maedhros had died and Maglor had disappeared forever.[4] Meanwhile, the War of Wrath played out

---

4. Stepping back a moment, what separation from caregivers at fifty-five years old means to two Peredhil who are 62% non-Edain is unclear. Eärendil and Elwing were 50% and 25% Mannish, respectively, and at 29 years old they were not only parents but leaders of their folk, which is significant, as the highly debated essay Laws and Customs Among the Eldar asserts that Eldar come of age around 50, and finish maturing by 100. Therefore, whether Elrond and Elros's separation from caregivers would be considered markedly traumatic or particularly salient for identity and development at fifty-five

and Beleriand was destroyed, after which Elrond chose to live as an Elf, and Elros chose the fate of Men. By Second Age (S.A.) 32 Elros became the first king of Númenor. Elrond was involved in several wars, including the Last Alliance, where he fought alongside many of his relatives and saw many of them fall. During the final attack on Barad-dûr, both Gil-galad (a potential mentor) and Elendil – a descendent of Elros – died while opposing Sauron. Soon Isildur would die, too, leaving his one remaining son, Valandil, in Elrond's care.

2.2 - Why Does This Matter?: Breaking the Cycle of Intergenerational Trauma

Family history matters, per Tolkien's universe and research in human development. While some of Elrond's sunnier life outcomes may be correlated with the timing of various retreats and his gaining of Vilya, his life is by no means unmarked by suffering – none of his family before him survived intact. For whatever reason – whether it was the love that grew between Maglor and the children, or the assumed comradeship he found with Gil-galad thereafter – *something* buffered Elrond from the fates of so many of his ancestors.

But there is more that makes Elrond's legacy relevant. Elrond not only demonstrates remarkable resilience, but he cultivates compassion and lives it. Elrond and Elros's early years were traumatic and chaotic – they were born refugees and, for a not insignificant amount of time, remained so. Nevertheless, both established realms of a sort. However, Elrond's establishment of Imladris as a stronghold against Sauron around S.A. 1697 would prove to be somewhat more symbolic. Although

depends much on the implications of their maturity. Loss is, however, still loss, and it may exacerbate already existing trauma-related issues.

Imladris was besieged, it became an intentionally constructed haven for displaced elves. Elven refugees flocked to Imladris and, eventually, Elrond used Vilya – gifted him by Gil-galad – to protect Imladris and make it the Last Homely House so familiar to readers.[5]

From Sirion – a land of multiple peoples, races, and ethnicities, displaced and, then, destroyed together – to Imladris – a land of refugees from Beleriand and then Eregion, where all are welcome regardless of race or need – the peoples of Middle-earth persevere. And so, the burnt hand – and the burnt hands of Elrond's diverse and storied kin – does, in fact, teach most about fire. In this case, the elves' obsession with "hoarding memory" is not a detriment. It is rather *because* of these memories that havens rise elsewhere, for Elrond is – first and foremost – a healer and a loremaster. It is in that haven of Imladris that Elrond will foster and protect the sons of his brother's line, and it will be the rejoining of these lines – with the history of his and Elros's legacies stretched like a finally healed wound between them – that facilitates the reunification of Middle-earth.

---

5. Vilya itself comes full circle from both a narrative and family trauma perspective – the quests for the Silmirilli which had sown distrust between the elves and other races, allowing Morgoth and Sauron to take hold – a quest which Celebrimbor, son of Celegorm forsook – led to the establishment of Celebrimbor in Eregion, where he would meet Sauron as Annatar, who would teach him how to forge the rings which would, ultimately, enable resistance to Sauron and, partially, facilitate his downfall. These rings would be carried by a descendent of Fëanor's half-brother (Gil-galad), by a Teleri elf (Cirdan), by an elf who witnessed two or more of the Kinslayings by the hands of her very own kin (Galadriel), by a true if hidden emissary of the Valar (Gandalf), and by Elrond.

3 - Consequences of Resettlement: The "Sindarizing" of the "Wild," "Lesser"[6] Elves by the Sindarin Princes and Noldorin Exiles of Beleriand

While Elrond constructed a new refuge and stronghold, the "Sindarin princes of the Silvan elves" resettled in already existing wood-elven regions East of the Mountains: Mirkwood and Lothlórien (*UT*, 270). Though the Sindar and Noldor who ultimately settled there were pushed to migrate due to the destruction of Beleriand, first, and the specific destruction of Eregion, second, their motivations for original migration were mixed. Whether due to trauma exposure or original cultural differences, linguistic clues suggest that settlement may have progressed differently in Lórien than in Mirkwood. This exploration demonstrates the potential effects of displacement across cultures.

3.1 - Brief Contextual Overview

While this paper is not the place to explore the implied ethnic and cultural Elven hierarchies, this section does require consideration of the delineation between elves who did and did not successfully follow the original call to Valinor. Within Tolkien's elven worlds,[7] these hierarchies are governed by (a) proximity to Aman and the Valar and, within Middle-earth, (b) proximity to the Noldor, with the Nandor and then the Avari being most distant.[8] Characteristic phrases used to describe

---

6. *UT*, 108, 248; *Letters*, Letter 144, 176.

7. At least as presented by the texts' largely Noldorin, in-universe narrators.

8. There is, arguably, further differentiation within the Nandor, with the Silvans east of the mountains – the interest of this paper – relatively lower in esteem than the laiquendi and guest-elves of Beleriand (who, at least for a time, fought or lived alongside the Sindar and Noldor).

the Silvan and Avari are "lesser Elves," "lesser Silvan race," "wild," "savage," "rude and rustic," and "more dangerous, less wise."[9] Given this language, it would be both easy and defensible to take a strictly colonial lens to these relationships. However, in the contexts presented in this paper, it would be somewhat disingenuous. When people are violently displaced, they must resettle, and *that* is what this section of the paper seeks to understand.

Lastly, it would be irresponsible not to acknowledge that information on everything having to do with the wood-elves (including Galadriel herself) is simultaneously scarce and contradictory. Christopher Tolkien opens Galadriel and Celeborn's essay in *Unfinished Tales* thusly: "There is no part of the history of Middle-earth more full of problems than the story of Galadriel and Celeborn" (239). And while much has been written in scholarly circles about Tolkien's languages and their relationships in-universe generally, the issue of language and culture as it pertains to a subset of the Teleri (the wood-elves) has been unexplored in publication (though it is worth noting that discussion is alive and well – if contentious – in fan communities). Of the non-Sindar Teleri and Avari, Tolkien himself writes in a pre-*Lord of the Rings* letter from 1954, "The lesser Elves hardly appear [in my work], except as part of the people of The Elf-realm; of Northern Mirkwood, and of Lórien, ruled by Eldar; their languages do not appear" (*Letters*, Letter 144, 174), and this remains almost entirely true, even through Christopher Tolkien's publications over the next several decades.

---

9. *Letters*, Letter 144, 176; *UT*, 108, 260, 272; *Silmarillion*, 94; *Hobbit*, 'Flies and Spiders', 164.

3.1.1 - Language as a Cultural Indicator of Differing Resettlement Processes

In this section, language is the cultural indicator of differing resettlement processes. Even disparate fields of study regard language as intrinsic to ethnic and cultural identity, and loss of language is often associated with displacement and colonization. Languages' association with national identity was particularly poignant during the time periods in which Tolkien himself began writing (Fimi 2018, 16), though nationalism's sway over Tolkien's own motivations certainly diminished over time (Fimi 2010, 61). While Tolkien had an interest in invented languages long before developing his legendarium and while the belief long persisted that he only built Middle-earth to sate a desire to situate his languages in something compelling and concrete, scholar Dimitra Fimi's now seminal *Tolkien, Race and Cultural History* (2008) effectively argues that both language and mythology developed independently until (per Tolkien's own admission in Letter 144) they became interconnected, "[flowing] together" and "integrally related" (66). While language everywhere has power, this tightly interwoven origin story of language, history, and culture – a simultaneous development with constantly interacting influence, evident in writings through the end of his life – positions language in Middle-earth as particularly symbolic. Ultimately, language in the legendarium is used both as an *explicit* cultural weapon (e.g., Thingol's ban on the use of Quenya in Beleriand) and an assumptively *implicit* one, with Sindarin subsuming Nandorin in most regions by the end of the T.A.[10]

10. However, how that subsuming happens is hotly contested in fan communities, and for good reason: Across his decades of writing Tolkien gives at least three differing accounts of Nandorin and Silvan in T.A. Middle-

3.2 - Social Ecological Models: Hypothesizing the Why

Because there is so little consistent information on elven resettlement, it is necessary to lean on the temporal and cultural aspects of our social ecological framework to understand the implied differences between Lothlórien and Mirkwood. While Galadriel was the first recorded to make contact with the Nandor, Amdír was king in Lórien and Oropher in Mirkwood.[11] Both were, however, Sindarin, with at least Oropher and Thranduil explicitly originating in Doriath. It is therefore reasonable to make some assumptions about the impact of their experiences. In some of his last writings on Oropher and Thranduil, Tolkien explicitly writes that "they did not wish to be merged with the other Sindar of Beleriand [in Lórien], dominated by the Noldorin Exiles for whom the folk of Doriath

─────────────────────────────

earth (an evolution that is the purview of a separate paper). However, given Tolkien's thoughts on the pleasure to be found in language diversity, it is entirely unsurprising that his thoughts on language among the T.A. Elves of the T.A. developed over time. After all, in a letter to his son in 1943, he emphatically wrote: "⅛ of the world's population speaks 'English', and that is the biggest language group. If true, damn shame – say I. May the curse of Babel strike all their tongues till they can only say 'baa baa'. It would mean much the same. I think I shall have to refuse to speak anything but Old Mercian" (Letter 53, 65).

11. While defining royalty in Noldorin lines is fairly straightforward, we are given no real instruction regarding the Sindar in Middle-earth. Therefore, what "Sindarin princes" means is undefined. It might mean that Amdír and Oropher were bloodkin to Thingol of Doriath; were in some way elevated in Sindarin courts prior to migration; or were, alternatively, accepted as leaders after migration. We do not know.

Unfortunately, Amdír is mentioned far fewer times in the legendarium than his son Amroth (in large part, one assumes, due to Tolkien's original construction of Amroth as a son of Galadriel), so we know very little about him.

had no great love" (*UT*, 272).[12] The memory of elves is long and, for whatever reason, the Kinslayings at Doriath and Sirion seem to have been more salient to Oropher and Thranduil than to the eventual Sindar of Lórien.[13]

The implied ethnic makeup of Lórien and Mirkwood may explain some differences in settlement behavior. While Tolkien describes Mirkwood as being almost entirely Silvan even after the Sindar's resettlement, Lothlórien had far more Sindarin and Noldorin refugees from Eregion than did Mirkwood. Although there is conflicting information on the Silvan language, one of Tolkien's final philological writings explains that Oropher and the few Sindarin refugees with him assimilated entirely into Silvan culture, "adopting their language and taking names of Silvan form and style" (272), which we see in the name of Oropher's grandson, Legolas, a "dialectical" form of the more traditional and "pure" Sindarin *laegolas* (*Letters*, Letter 211, 282).[14] A 1972 letter states that the elves of Thranduil's realm did not, in fact, speak Sindarin at all – as originally stated in *The Lord of the Rings* appendices decades before – but a "related language or dialect" (*Letters*, Letter 347, 425). This is in contrast to the Silvans of Lórien, as another essay from the same time period declared the elves of Lórien all

---

12. Presumably because they had been directly displaced by the Kinslayings at Doriath in F.A. 506 and, likely, again as refugees at Sirion in F.A. 538. The Kinslaying at Sirion left few alive, meaning it is not unlikely that (if present) they may have been some of the only survivors.

13. If Amdír and Amroth were originally Northern Sindarin, however, and had had early, extended contact with the Noldor and Fëanorians via Hithlum/Mithrim as opposed to Gondolin or Doriath, this might easily explain some of those differences, as they would not have been directly affected by the Kinslayings in Doriath or Sirion. However, we simply-from the text-cannot know.

14. Of note, "ae" is only used on one occasion in the remnants of Nandorin Tolkien provides. All others are either "a" or "e".

Sindarin-speakers (although the language they spoke amongst themselves might have been Silvan-influenced) (*UT*, 269).[15]

Ultimately, the Sindar and Noldor of Lórien appear to have merged less with the native Silvan than did the Sindar of Mirkwood,[16] though the perspectives of wood-elves themselves are woefully underrepresented in the legendarium. Apart from Legolas (who, regardless of his debatable "royal and *originally* Sindarin" ancestry, self-identifies as Silvan), and a few guards, the only *truly* Silvan perspective in all of Tolkien's writings is that of Nimrodel, a Silvan Elf of Lórien (emphasis mine, *Letters*, Letter 297, 382). Nimrodel's feelings on the Noldorin-Sindarin resettlement and the subsequent dilution of Silvan culture (even thousands of years after initial contact) provide insights into the disruption of native life in Lórien. Of her, Tolkien writes: "She [...] regretted the incoming of the Elves from the West, who (as she said) brought wars and destroyed the peace of old. She would speak only the Silvan tongue, even after it had fallen into disuse among the folk of Lórien" (*UT*, 252). Curiously, even though Amroth merges with Silvan culture (which he did "because of his love for Nimrodel," (282)) and the name he uses is Silvan-influenced, there is a repeatedly stated loss of language in Lórien.

It is possible that diverse reasons for migration (outside of refugee-related flight) complicate these outcomes. While some of the Noldor returned to Valinor at the end of the F.A., some later settled in Lórien. However, Galadriel's *initial* motivation

---

15. Which, again, contradicts some of his earlier writing in *The Lord of the Rings* and the Appendices, indicating that his in-world views evolved over time.

16. Of course, this perception could be due to Tolkien writing more explicitly about the Silvan language in Mirkwood in his later years than in Lórien, for Galadriel ever dominated his thoughts there.

for migrating from Valinor complicates matters, for she first thought to leave Valinor before any of the discontent. Later, though she swore no oaths, "the words of Fëanor concerning Middle-earth had kindled in her heart, for she yearned to see the wide unguarded lands and *to rule there a realm at her own will*" (emphasis mine, *Silmarillion*, 93). Upon arriving in Middle-earth, however, Galadriel missed Valinor and reminisced often. Still, she specifically eschewed some memories of the past, as when Melian pressed her about Alqualondë: "[T]hat woe is past,' said Galadriel; 'and I would take what joy is left here, untroubled by memory'" (151).

However, like Oropher, Galadriel does not leave memory behind. When she does eventually settle permanently in Lórien, Tolkien writes that: "[s]he had endeavoured to make Lórien a refuge and an island of peace and beauty, *a memorial of ancient days*" (emphasis mine, *UT*, 265). Further, Tolkien's conception of the origin of the name "Lórien" changes over time and across narrators. The original name of Lothlórien was allegedly "Lindórinand," a word of Nandorin (Silvan) origin referencing the word they used to refer to themselves (in Nandorin, the *Lindi*) and roughly translating to "Vale of the Land of the Singers." Another possible Nandorin name for Lothlórien is "Lórinand," or "Valley of Gold" – whether this name emerged among the Silvan prior to or after contact is unclear (265). What is clear, however, is that at some point the "original and ancient Nandorin name of the region" was adapted, influenced by Sindarin and Quenya roots to form the names with which we are most familiar: Lórien and Lothlórien (265). Tolkien highlights the names' post-contact connection to Valinor repeatedly; and Christopher writes, "it emerges that all the later names [after contact] were probably due to Galadriel herself" (265).

While Galadriel's power and experience as a High Elf is uncontestable, the influence of the Noldor in Lórien is undeniable.[17] While Oropher and Thranduil's experiences created memories that drove them to distance themselves from High-Elven influence and thus preserve-even incidentally-the cultural identity of the native wood-elves, the impact of Amdír and Amroth's experiences are unclear. Even experiences that might have resulted in similar cultural outcomes to Mirkwood leadership seem to have been mitigated by the influence of a larger Sindarin and Noldorin population in Lórien. While Galadriel demonstrates growth in regards to dominion during 'The Mirror of Galadriel', her initial motivation for migration from Valinor to Middle-earth alters the sociohistorical setting and, thus, the lenses through which we approach Lórien's culture. While Tolkien considered the High Elves the most noble of the Eldar,[18] it is, arguably, the Silvan realm most uninfluenced by the Sindar and Noldor whose resettlement leads to the more noble treatment of the native folk.[19]

Of course, like all things Tolkien, the cycle does not end there. Much like Elrond's story, the legacy of Elven Sundering, of violence and displacement, and of the increasing distance and isolation between the wood-elven realms is fated (by the end of the T.A.) to resolve. At the height of the War of the Ring, Celeborn and Galadriel fight the forces of evil in Dol Guldur in southern Mirkwood while Thranduil defends the North. Though Mirkwood burns despite victory, Celeborn and Thranduil meet

---

17. And her elven ring ultimately protects the Silvan folk of Lórien (and, per some evidence, may have preserved certain linguistic traditions that developed during their isolation after the War of the Last Alliance and, again, after the Balrog was awoken and Amroth was lost around T.A. 1981.)

18. And had envisioned them as such since their very awakening at Cuiviénen.

19. Or, at the least, to the preservation of their language and culture upon initial contact.

to reunite the sundered woodland realms as Eryn Lasgalen and East Lórien, and the wood is lifted out of darkness. A few years later, when the preservation of Lórien crumbles – after Galadriel herself leaves for Valinor, after Celeborn moves to Imladris to live with Elrond's sons – elves continue to make East Lórien (in the South of Mirkwood) and Eryn Lasgalen their homes. Meanwhile, even farther south, a son of Mirkwood (Legolas, who stood and survived with a descendent of Elros on that very field that felled his own grandfather millennia before) establishes a community of wood-elves in Gondor's Ithilien – a community of service, where elves would work with dwarves and Men to heal a shared land, and to mend what was burnt.

Tolkien once wrote that for stories to be successful "there must be some relevance to the 'human situation' (of all periods)" (*Letters*, Letter 181, 233). Refugees, displacement narratives, and experiences of trauma in our contemporary world are just as relevant – and prevalent – today as they were when Tolkien was writing. A range of peoples within Tolkien's Middle-earth experience trauma and displacement, just as people in our modern world. Tolkien's characters similarly react to it diversely, resulting in unique outcomes across social ecological levels with unique implications for history, wellbeing, and culture. The applicability of Tolkien's writing to current global experiences is, in fact, increasingly relevant, as 2022 saw the largest number of displaced persons since the United Nations began tracking displacement (100 million worldwide), and current conflict in Ukraine has created the largest and most rapid refugee crisis the world has seen since Tolkien's own lifetime, in World War II (United Nations High Commissioner for Refugees 2022).

While Tolkien routinely eschewed allegory, he never did applicability: "That there is no allegory," he wrote, "does

not, of course, say there is no applicability. There always is"
(*Letters*, Letter 203, 262). Thus, equally applicable to our
understanding of Tolkien's works is our ability to use alternate
scientific and theoretical lenses to enrich our understanding of
his world, ultimately honoring his legacy by giving name to
themes we did not, before, have the language to meaningfully
explore. Utilizing modern knowledge of trauma and its impacts
within a social ecological framework allows us to mine fresh
insights from timeless works and apply them within the
framework of our modern context. Furthermore, what are
today's current events will one day be memory, as complex
as the tales analyzed in this paper and, likely, as evanescent.
A trauma-informed social ecological framework helps us to
comprehend and give weight to the *context* of experience and
the time and place in which memories are made and individuals
are affected. Ultimately, from Elrond to Galadriel to Thranduil
– through all their family trees and back again – it is safe to
conclude that the burnt hand does, in fact, teach most about
fire, even as embedded as each individual's memories are in
their cultural and historical contexts.

Bibliography

Bryant, Richard; Ben, Edwards; Creamer, Mark; O'Donnell, Meaghan; Forbes, David; Felmingham, Kim; Silove, Derrick; Steel, Zachary; Nickerson, Angela; McFarlane, Alexander; Van Hoof, Miranda; and Hadzi-Pavlovic, Dusan, 'The effect of post-traumatic stress disorder on refugees' parenting and their children's mental health: a cohort study', *The Lancet Public Health*, 3.5 (2018), 249–58 <https://doi.org/10.1016/S2468-2667(18)30051-3>

Cobham, Vanessa and Newnham, Elizabeth, 'Trauma and Parenting: Considering Humanitarian Crisis Contexts', in *Handbook of Parenting and Child Development Across the Lifespan* (Springer International Publishing, 2020), pp. 143-169.

Drury, John and Williams, Richard, 'Children and young people who are refugees, internally displaced persons or survivors or perpetrators of war, mass violence and terrorism', *Current Opinion in Psychiatry*, 25.4 (2012), 227-84 <https://doi.org/10.1097/YCO.0b013e328353eea6>

Fimi, Dimitra, *Tolkien, Race and Cultural History: From Fairies to Hobbits*, (London: Palgrave Macmillan, 2010).
--- 'Language as Communication vs. Language as Art: J.R.R. Tolkien and early 20th-century radical linguistic experimentation," *Journal of Tolkien Research*, 5.1 (2018)

Greenberg, David; Baron-Cohen, Simon; Rosenberg, Nora; Fonagy, Peter; and Rentfrow, Peter, 'Elevated empathy in adults following childhood trauma', *PLoS ONE*, 13.10 (2018), < https://doi.org/10.1371/journal.pone.0203886>

International Society for Traumatic Stress Studies, *Trauma During Adulthood*, online fact sheet, no date, <https://istss.org/public-resources/trauma-basics/trauma-during-adulthood> [accessed 8 May 2021].

Isobel, Sophie; Goodyear, Melinda; Furness, Thentham; and Foster, Kim, 'Preventing intergenerational trauma transmission: A critical interpretive synthesis', *Journal of Clinical Nursing*, 28.7 (2018), 1100-13 < https://doi.org/10.1111/jocn.14735>

Lounsbury, David and Mitchell, Shannon, 'Introduction to special issue on social ecological approaches to community health research and action',

American Journal of Community Psychology, 44.3 (2009), 213-20 <https://doi.org/10.1007/s10464-009-9266-4>

Luthar, Suniya, Cicchetti, Dante and Becker, Bronwyn, 'The construct of resilience: A critical evaluation and guidelines for future work', *Child Development*, 71.3 (2003), 543-62 <https://doi.org/10.1111/1467-8624.00164>

Masten, Ann and Narayan, Angela, 'Child development in the context of disaster, war, and terrorism: Pathways of risk and resilience', *Annual Review of Psychology*, 63 (2012), 227-57 < https://doi.org/10.1146/annurev-psych-120710-100356>

Morelli, Nicholas; Duong, Jacqueline; Evans, Meghan; Hong, Kajyung; Garcia, Jackelyne; Ogbonnaya, Ijeoma; and Villodas, Miguel, 'Intergenerational Transmission of Abusive Parenting: Role of Prospective Maternal Distress and Family Violence', *Child Maltreatment*, 26.2 (2021), 172-81 <https://doi.org/10.1177/1077559520947816>

Patel, Sita; Staudenmeyer, Anna; Wickama, Robert; Firmender, William; Fields, Laurie; and Miller, Alisa, 'War-exposed newcomer adolescent immigrants facing daily life stressors in the United States', *International Journal of Intercultural Relations*, 60 (2017), 120-31 <https://doi.org/10.1016/j.ijintrel.2017.03.002>

Schauer, Maggie, Neuner, Frank and Elbert, Thomas, *Narrative Exposure Therapy: A short-term intervention for traumatic stress disorders after war, terror, or torture*. (Gottingen: Hogrefe & Huber Publishers, 2005).

Tolkien, J.R.R, *The Lord of the Rings*, (London: George Allen & Unwin, 1969).
--- *The Hobbit*, (New York: Ballantine Books, 1976).
--- *The Silmarillion*, ed. by Christopher Tolkien (London: George Allen & Unwin, 1977).
--- *Unfinished Tales: The Lost Lore of Middle-earth*, ed. by Christopher Tolkien (New York: Random House Publishing Group, 1988).
--- *The Peoples of Middle-earth*, ed. by Christopher Tolkien (London: HarperCollins, 1996; Boston: Houghton Mifflin, 1996)
--- *The Letters of J.R.R. Tolkien*, ed. by Humphrey Carpenter with the assistance of Christopher Tolkien (Boston: Houghton Mifflin Harcourt, 2000).

United Nations High Commissioner for Refugees, *Global Displacement Hits Another Record Capping Decade Long Rising Trend*, 16 June 2022, < https://www.unhcr.org/en-us/news/press/2022/6/62a9d2b04/unhcr-global-displacement-hits-record-capping-decade-long-rising-trend.html> [accessed 5 January 2022].

Vollhardt, Johanna and Staub, Ervin, 'Inclusive altruism born of suffering: The relationship between adversity and prosocial attitudes and behavior toward disadvantaged outgroups', *American Journal of Orthopsychiatry*, 81.3 (2011), 307-15, <https://doi.org/10.1111/j.1939-0025.2011.01099.x>

Appendix

Elrond and Elros: Tracing Generational Trauma
Elwing's Family

Elwing is a refugee of Doriath when the children are born in F.A. 532. Her mother and father Dior and Nimloth, rulers of Doriath, were slain by the sons of Fëanor during the same event from which she fled with a Silmaril: the Second Kinslaying in F.A. 506, when Elwing was about three years old. Elwing's siblings Eluréd and Elurín, also children at the time, were left to die by Feanorians during the event. While Nimloth's history is relatively unknown, Dior's parents Lúthien and Beren had already died once – following a Silmaril-related incident – from, respectively, grief and violent injury. After being granted life a second time, Lúthien gave birth to Dior; later, they were presumed dead with the return of the Silmaril to Doriath in F.A. 503. Beren himself had, as a young man, been a refugee with a group of men and his father following the Dagor Bragollach – he returned after a mission to find his father and kinsmen slaughtered by the forces of Morgoth in, what is implied by Tolkien, a fairly disturbing manner ("blood dripped from [the] beaks [of the carrion]" (*Silmarillion*, 197). He dealt with their bodies and then wandered alone for years (pursued intermittently) until eventually arriving in Doriath, where he would meet Lúthien and begin his quest for a Silmaril.

Lúthien's parents, of course, are Thingol and Melian. Thingol had been a leader of elves during the first great Sundering, but had been delayed in the journey when he and Melian – a Maia, one of the Ainur – met in the woods of Nan Elmoth, at which point Thingol was sundered from his brother Olwe, who became a leader of the Teleri in Valinor. Eventually, Thingol and Melian established Doriath, and Melian protected it. Like most elves in Beleriand at the time, Thingol was exposed to traumatic events in the form of battles and loss, which culminated in his death at the hands of the dwarves following a

Silmaril-related incident. Melian then returned to Valinor, leaving Doriath unprotected, and the folk of Doriath endured the Battle of Ten Thousand Caves in Menegroth (F.A. 503).

Eärendil's Family

Eärendil is a refugee of Gondolin who traveled with his parents after its destruction by Morgoth's forces in F.A. 510. Eärendil was not only exposed to that horrific battle at seven years old, witnessing the destruction of his home, but he was also threatened with death by his mother's cousin, Maeglin, and witnessed Maeglin's attempt on his mother's life, and his subsequent demise. He then fled with his folk, ending up with his mother and father at the Mouths of Sirion, where Elwing's people already dwelt. Idril and Tuor would sail West in F.A. 525, and Eärendil would lead the folk then, though he was often away due to Sea-longing.

After the First Kinslaying, the stealing of the ships at Alqualonde, and the murder of her great grandfather Finwe by Morgoth, Idril crossed the Helcaraxë with her parents Turgon and Elenwë, led by her grandfather Fingolfin, whose wife stayed behind. Many elves – including Idril's mother Elenwë – died in the crossing, which was filled of "hardihood" and "woe," and Idril herself was almost lost in the "cruel sea," saved by her father even as her mother was lost (*Silmarillion*, 102; *Peoples*, 415). Turgon's life was not a particularly happy one. Soon after arriving in Middle-earth, he begins to build Gondolin in secret. In F.A. 400, his sister Aredhel was murdered in front of him (to which he responded by throwing Eöl off a cliff). Turgon's father Fingolfin died in F.A. 456, after challenging Morgoth to a duel – it was Turgon who buried his father's broken body. Finally, in F.A. 472, Turgon led a host of his people from Gondolin to support the alliance of men, dwarves, and elves – including his brother Fingon – at the Battle of Unnumbered Tears. There, Turgon saw his brother hewn by Gothmog, and returned to Gondolin with lesser forces as the High King of the Noldor, the last of his siblings.

The trauma associated with Fingolfin and its ripple effects not just through Finwean family history but the entirety of Arda is worth mentioning here. The relationship between Fingolfin and his half-brother Fëanor is rather famously stressed, as Fëanor resented the loss of his mother and his father's remarriage. Fingolfin is threatened by his half-brother Fëanor on multiple occasions, and then betrayed by him as they come upon the Helcaraxe, a betrayal that ends in the loss of many of their folk, regardless of the Fëanorians initial defeat of Morgoth while Fingolfin labored across the Helcaraxë. Fingolfin dies after a solitary assault upon Morgoth after he wrongly believes all his folk have been destroyed in the Dagor Bragollach.

Tuor's family, to say nothing of the tragedy of his uncle Húrin's line, is also, unsurprisingly, marked by loss. Tuor's grandfather Galdor is slain in the Dagor Bragollach. Rían was a refugee during and, presumably, after the Dagor Bragollach, separated from, at least, her father. Rían and Huor marry shortly before the Battle of Unnumbered Tears, and then they conceive Tuor. However, before Tuor is even born, Huor is slain, and his mother – not knowing her husband's fate – lives long enough to birth Tuor, before fostering him to the elves and dying of grief. For sixteen years, Tuor lived in an occupied land with Annael and the elven refugees from Mithrim, until they attempted to flee to the Mouths of Sirion in F.A. 488. However, they were attacked by orcs, and Tuor was ultimately separated from his folk and taken in thrall by the Easterlings, where he was tormented until he escaped at nineteen. He continued to live as a refugee and "outlaw" for several years until being guided by Ulmo to the hidden city of Gondolin, where he would meet and marry Idril. Their son Eärendil (the father of Elrond and Elros) would be born in F.A. 503, seven years before the fall of Gondolin.

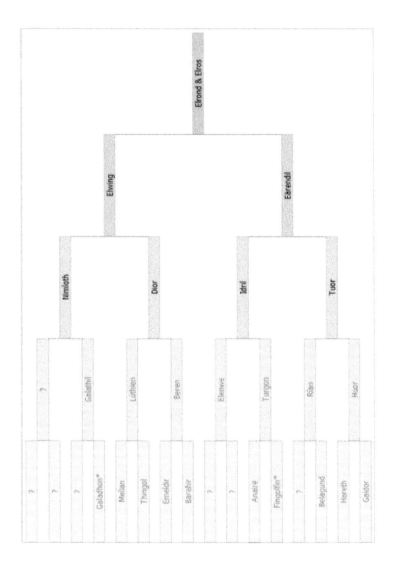

The Problem of Pain: Portraying Physical Disability in the Fantasy of J.R.R. Tolkien

Clare Moore

Disability scholars have long noted the abundance of disabled characters in literature, from ancient myths to the most contemporary of novels, characters who portray a wide variety of physical and intellectual disabilities. This established presence and diversity of disability is as apparent in Middle-earth as it is in any other literary tradition. Tolkien's legendarium features a plethora of characters who exhibit different disabilities, from Niënor's memory loss in *The Silmarillion* to perhaps Tolkien's most famous example of Frodo in *The Lord of the Rings*. Several scholars have examined disability in Tolkien's work, but most scholarship focuses on Frodo, such as Michael Livingston's 'The Shell-shocked Hobbit', Anna Smol's 'Frodo's Body', and Verlyn Flieger's 'The Body in Question', which analyze Frodo's physical and psychological injuries in light of Tolkien's experience in World War I. Studies focused on characters from *The Silmarillion*, such as Irina Metzler's 'Tolkien and disability' and Victoria Wodzak's 'Tolkien's Gimpy Heroes', approach Tolkien's portrayal of disabled characters through a strict social model of disability.

The social model has predominantly influenced modern disability studies and asserts that disability is the result of a non-normative body engaging in a world engineered for "normate" bodies (Mollow 2017, 342). A prime example of this is a wheelchair user encountering stairs. The stairs were designed and built for specific bodies, but access is easily granted to a different type of body by building a ramp. The focus of this model, then, is to acknowledge that the problems that arise from disability are the result of societal constructs based on a specific view of what 'normal' bodies should be able to do, and this counteracts the earlier medical model of disability theory.

The medical model of disability views physical or intellectual impairments as the cause of limitations for disabled people (342). Therefore, it is not the stairs that are the problem, but the person's legs, which do not function as they should – according to a medical model. Many disabled people and scholars object to this view because it is based on the premise that there is something *wrong* with a disabled person, and not just different. Recently, however, scholars and disabled people have argued that the strict social model does not present a comprehensive view of disability because it threatens to erase the body by focusing on social environments and not the physical experience of disability.

Disability covers a wide range of conditions and experiences, some of which involve more physical experiences than others. Often, depending on the disability, this physical experience involves momentary or chronic pain, but both the social and medical model of disability have not reconciled where pain fits in the disabled experience, how it factors into our understanding of what it can mean to be disabled, how to incorporate it into advocacy, and how to portray pain in representations of disability in literature.

This paper will examine how Tolkien portrays physical pain in *The Silmarillion* and *The Lord of the Rings* through the characters of Maedhros, Beren, Morgoth, and Frodo as a case study in one author's representation of pain-as-tied-to-disability in literature. Because the term disability can apply to so many conditions, I will narrow this analysis down to physical disabilities caused by injuries received during a character's physical and narrative maturity. Beren, Maedhros, Morgoth, and Frodo all receive physical injuries as adults, during the unfolding of their primary narratives, and experience injuries that would undeniably cause physical pain at the time of occurrence and afterwards.

The study of these characters reveals that Tolkien accounts for the physical pain his characters experience when they receive their injuries but he does not focus on a vivid portrayal of pain as part of the lived experience of disability after the injury has occurred. When Tolkien does offer a sustained account of the experience of disability after the fact, physical pain is inherently tied to, and predominantly subsumed into, the experience of psychological and spiritual pain.

Tolkien describes the physical pain of each of the four above characters at the moment they receive their injuries in varying detail. Maedhros, hanging from a precipice of Thangorodrim by an iron cuff around his wrist, is in enough pain that he begs Fingon to kill him (*Silmarillion*, 110). Fingon, however, severs his hand from his arm, but Tolkien does not include any descriptions of the resulting pain of this act, only writing that Fingon cut off Maedhros' hand and Thorondor the eagle bore them away (110). There is nothing to suggest that Tolkien is denying what can only be an intensely painful physical experience, but in the case of Maedhros Tolkien does not vividly portray the pain associated with having a hand severed from the body. The loss of Beren's hand is very similar. Tolkien describes the pain Carcharoth experiences as the Silmaril burns inside him, but regarding Beren Tolkien writes only that Beren "swooned" (182). There is no accompanying explicit account of the pain of having a wolf bite off his hand with venomous fangs, despite Beren being described as near to death.

In *The Silmarillion*, Tolkien's most direct description of physical pain at the moment of injury occurs when Fingolfin wounds Morgoth. Tolkien writes that Fingolfin "wounded Morgoth with seven wounds, and seven times Morgoth gave a cry of anguish" (154). In this scene, Morgoth's cries of anguish are a physical reaction to the pain caused by his injury. This might seem an obvious thing to state, but it will become more singular upon the analysis of the dominant connection between physical injury and psychological pain, which I will address in a moment.

Frodo receives multiple physical injuries during his narrative. When the Witch-King stabs him on Weathertop, "he felt a great pain like a dart of poisoned ice pierce his left shoulder" (*FR*, 'A Knife in the Dark', 191). Like Morgoth when Fingolfin stabs his foot, Frodo's pain is explicit at the moment the Witch-King wounds him. The pain of losing his finger to Gollum's teeth is likewise hinted at through a cry (*FR*, 'Mount Doom', 925). However, Tolkien does not portray Shelob's attack on Frodo in Cirith Ungol. Sam finds him unconscious and already wounded (*TT*, 'The Choices of Master Samwise', 713). Frodo, therefore, represents Tolkien's differing approaches to portraying pain at the time of injury. Sometimes physical pain is explicit, sometimes implied, and other times brushed over.

There are narrative reasons for Tolkien to vary his approach. For example, it is an effective narrative strategy for the reader to leave Frodo unharmed and to then discover his unconscious body along with Sam as narrator, creating suspense and surprise for the reader. However, it is still of note that while Tolkien never seems to deny the pain of injury, his depictions of it are usually one sentence at most. He does not linger on the moment or its experience. This, too, has narrative practicality, especially in *The Silmarillion*, which by its nature is more summary in style than *The Lord of the Rings*, and Tolkien handles many different types of dramatic moments in the narrative with the same efficient manner he uses in portraying moments of pain. But this does raise the question of how much space in the narrative pain should occupy, and continue to occupy, after the moment of injury has passed.

Though Tolkien does not erase or even mitigate the reality of pain from physical injury, he does not focus on any sustained accounts of physical pain *after* the moment of injury for characters in *The Silmarillion*. That is not to say that he does not acknowledge the fact that disabilities caused by physical injuries can result in chronic pain or in moments of pain experienced later, but it is never the focus of a character's narrative. If there is continued suffering that results from the injuries sustained by a character, it is almost always transformed into psychological pain. Maedhros is a prime example of this. Tolkien writes that Maedhros is healed following his injury and rescue, and that the "shadow of his pain was in his heart" (*Silmarillion*, 111). The language moves Maedhros' pain out of the physical realm and into the psychological, almost spiritual, realm of his heart.

There are no later hints that Maedhros suffers physically from the loss of his hand. In fact, after learning to wield a sword with his left hand better than his right, Maedhros seems to be *more* physically capable than ever before. Metzler writes that this is an example of overcoming or negating disability (2017, 42), but given the mythic nature of *The Silmarillion* and Tolkien's admiration and echoing of Norse mythology, there is another possible interpretation. In his essay 'From the Mute God to the Lesser God: Disability in Medieval Celtic and Old Norse literature', Lois Bragg writes that disability scholars often take their modern understanding of disability to premodern texts, that "what we call disabilities are perhaps always and everywhere exceptionalities, but not always disabilities" (1997, 165, 167). In analyzing specifical Icelandic texts, with which Tolkien was familiar, Bragg writes that what modern audiences would term physical disabilities are portrayed in Norse literature as impairments, or physical differences that alter the function of the body. They are mentioned and then rarely commented on again (172). This mirrors Tolkien's depiction of Maedhros's disability after the loss of his hand, and would explain the lack of a portrayal of a painful lived experience post-injury in the mythic stories of *The Silmarillion*.

With Beren, Tolkien sidesteps even the possibility of depicting the potential physical pain of a newly disabled life by having Beren die shortly after he receives his injury from Carcharoth. Much like Maedhros and the ancient northern heroic culture that inspired many of Tolkien's heroes, Beren's disability appears to be an impairment mentioned and then dropped, as Bragg suggests, but that is not necessarily a slight against Tolkien's story. In this case, it is narratively essential that Beren dies in order for this story to come to its glorious climax of Lúthien's song before Mandos, but nonetheless it is still another example of the absence of a portrayal of the lived experience of pain inherent in some physical disabilities.

As well as having the most direct connection between injury and physical pain, Morgoth also experiences the most physical pain post-injury in *The Silmarillion*. Unlike Maedhros and Beren, Morgoth's pain does not heal, and – unlike Maedhros – Morgoth's injury diminishes his physical ability, as he walks "ever halt of one foot after that day" (*Silmarillion*, 154). His pain remains physical, rather than becoming a 'shadow' in his heart, his status as a warrior decreasing. In this way, it is the villain of the narrative who exemplifies the most vivid and sustained experience of physical pain resulting from disability – a topic that certainly deserves its own paper.

In analyzing Frodo's post-injury experiences, it becomes necessary to introduce the tension between physical and psychological pain that occurs in Tolkien's writing. Tolkien does note purely physical pain after Frodo's multiple injuries. After being stabbed on Weathertop, Frodo's pain grows and spreads in his body, and *athelas* notably lessens the physical pain after the event (*FR*, 'Flight to the Ford', 194). Even after his healing in Rivendell, Frodo experiences pain on the journey back to the Shire and at home in Bag End again, both on the anniversary of the injury (*RK*, 'Homeward Bound', 967; 'The Grey Havens', 1001). These are examples of an undeniable physical experience, but it is impossible to completely disentangle the physical and psychological or even spiritual aspect of Frodo's disability and experience. Two of his injuries, the stab wound from the Witch-King and the loss of his finger, have undeniable symbolic meaning. This is noted by Metzler and expounded upon by Smol and Flieger, and so I do not intend to add commentary to the spiritual or psychological meaning of Frodo's physical experience. Rather, I want to call attention to the relationship between this well-noted symbolic interpretation and Tolkien's portrayal of physical pain.

Though Tolkien portrays the physical pain during and after Frodo's injuries, this pain is always tied to or, more often than not, subsumed by the symbolic meaning of Frodo's physicality. On the journey to Rivendell, the "cold and wet had made [Frodo's] wound more painful than ever", but Frodo "felt that black shapes were advancing to smother him' and 'a mist seemed to obscure his sight" (*FR*, 'Flight to the Ford', 197-9). Frodo's physical pain from the stab wound is always present simultaneously with a mist that darkens his sight and the feeling of approaching shadows. This spiritual wounding is heightened after Frodo's healing at Rivendell when Gandalf notes that "there was a faint change, just a hint as it were of transparency, about him, and especially about the left hand that lay outside the coverlet" (*FR*, 'Many Meetings', 217). All signs of physical pain are gone and only the shadow effect remains.

Frodo himself may explain this best when he tells Gandalf, "'There is no real going back. Though I may come to the Shire, it will not seem the same; for I shall not be the same. I am wounded with knife, sting, and tooth, and a long burden'" (*RK*, 'Homeward Bound', 967). It is not because of his scars or phantom physical pain that Frodo decides to sail to Valinor. It is his 'long burden' that continually affects him, as evidenced by his first illness in the Shire, which Frodo explains by saying, "It is gone forever [...] and now all is dark and empty" (*RK*, 'The Grey Havens', 1001). Frodo's lasting trauma is psychological and spiritual, despite the reality of the physicality of his injuries. In Frodo more than any other character, Tolkien integrates a dynamic experience of disability by incorporating the physical, psychological, and – for a devout Catholic – the spiritual pain that can result from specific injuries.

My analysis of the tension between the physical and psychological/spiritual/symbolic experience of pain in the character of Frodo is not a judgement call on Tolkien's portrayal. I hope none of the analyses in this paper are presented as judgments. Rather, I have attempted to draw out the facts of Tolkien's portrayal of pain in the characters of Maedhros, Beren, Morgoth, and Frodo in order to demonstrate that Tolkien did not shy away from depicting the pain of physical injuries, but he did not develop detailed portrayals of the continued lived experience of chronic pain. I do not think it was ever his intention to do so, and he had narrative reasons for structuring these portrayals as he did. I also believe Bragg's argument about Norse literature aligns with Tolkien's approach to presenting physical disability in the mythology of *The Silmarillion*. Likewise, though Frodo's physical pain is not primary in his experience, Tolkien does take it seriously. I also think that disability scholar Michael Bérubé is correct when he says that, contrary to previous disability theory approaches, literary representation must be allowed to be read as the site of the figural (Bérubé 2005, 570). It is essential to the story that Frodo's disability extends beyond the physical experience, but we as readers must not neglect the painful physical reality of Frodo's injuries.

Pain and disability can be difficult topics in life and literature, but Tolkien was willing to address such nuanced themes in his work. Physical pain is one aspect of some disabled experiences, one Tolkien did not deny in the lives of the characters who populated his Middle-earth, but there is still much work to be done on disability in Tolkien. It is my belief that this work will only deepen our understanding and appreciation of Tolkien's legendarium.

Bibliography

Bérubé, Michael, 'Disability and Narrative', *PMLA*, 120.2 (2005), 568-576.

Bragg, Lois, 'From the Mute God to the Lesser God: Disability in Medieval Celtic and Old Norse literature', *Disability and Society*, 12.2 (1997), 165-178.

Flieger, Verlyn, 'The Body in Question: The Unhealed Wounds of Frodo Baggins', in *The Body in Tolkien's Legendarium*, ed. by Christopher Vaccaro (Jefferson, NC: Macfarland & Company, Inc., Publishers, 2013), pp. 12-19.

Livingston, Michael, 'The Shell-shocked Hobbit: The First World War and Tolkien's Trauma of the Ring', *Mythlore*, 25.1 (2006), 77-92.

Metzler, Irina, 'Tolkien and disability: the narrative function of disabled characters in Middle-earth,' in *Death and Immortality in Middle-earth*, ed. by Daniel Helen (Edinburgh: Luna Press Publishing, 2017), pp. 35-50.

Mollow, Anna, 'Disability Studies', in *A Companion to Critical and Cultural Theory*, ed. by Imre Szeman, Sarah Blacker, and Justin Sully (Hoboken, NJ: John Wiley & Sons, Ltd, 2017), pp. 339-356.

Smol, Anna, 'Frodo's Body: Liminality and the Experience of War', in *The Body in Tolkien's Legendarium*, ed. by Christopher Vaccaro (Jefferson, NC: Macfarland & Company, Inc., Publishers, 2013), pp. 39-62.

Tolkien, J.R.R., *The Silmarillion*, ed. by Christopher Tolkien (New York: Houghton Mifflin, 1977).
--- *The Lord of the Rings* (New York: Houghton Mifflin, 1987).

Wodzak, Victoria Holtz, 'Tolkien's Gimpy Heroes', in *Mythlore*, 37.1 (2018), 103-118.

About the contributors

Sonali Arvind Chunodkar
Sonali Chunodkar is currently an independent researcher. Her M.Phil. thesis attempted a cognitive narratological examination of how Tolkien's narrative and stylistic choices are able to achieve secondary belief through the reader's co-creative activity. Her Ph.D. dissertation offered a Husserlian phenomenological investigation into the possibility of literary belief during the act of reading in general and that of reading Tolkien's fantasy fiction in particular. In addition to co-editing a volume on phenomenology, she is currently working on a paper that traces Tolkien's influence on select English-language mythological fantasy fiction produced in India since 2003.

Martha Celis-Mendoza
Martha Celis-Mendoza. Ph. D. in Hispanic Literature and M. A. in Translation, El Colegio de México. B. A. in English Literature, UNAM. Dissertation: Función de las Canciones de Poder en la obra de J.R.R. Tolkien. Diploma in Education of Virtues through Film, ULIA. COTE, Cambridge University. Head of the Translation Diploma Program, Universidad Iberoamericana. Lecturer in Translation and Comparative Literature (UNAM; Universidad Iberoamericana, AMETLI). Courses and papers on the life and works of J.R.R. Tolkien (The Anglo Mexican Foundation, CUIH, CENART). Book chapters and papers on Alfonso Reyes; Amparo Dávila; Mexican Women Translators; Translation Studies; Detective Stories; Shakespeare. Translator of scientific and literary texts.

Martha Celis-Mendoza. Doctora en Literatura Hispánica y Maestra en Traducción, El Colegio de México. Licenciada en Letras Inglesas, UNAM. Tesina: Función de las Canciones de Poder en la obra de J.R.R. Tolkien. Diplomado en Educación de las Virtudes a través del Cine, ULIA. COTE, Universidad de Cambridge. Coordinadora del Diplomado en Traducción, Universidad Iberoamericana. Profesora de Traducción y Literatura Comparada (UNAM; Universidad Iberoamericana, AMETLI, OMT, Universidad de Guanajuato). Cursos y ponencias sobre la vida y obra de J.R.R. Tolkien (The Anglo Mexican Foundation, CUIH, CENART). Capítulos de libros y ponencias sobre Alfonso Reyes; Amparo Dávila; traductoras mexicanas; Estudios de traducción; relato policial; Shakespeare. Traductora de textos científicos y literarios.

Robin Anne Reid

Robin Anne Reid is happily retired from her university position and continuing her scholarship as an independent scholar focusing on Tolkien, feminist science fiction and fantasy, and running the Tolkien Studies area at the Popular Culture conference for a few more years. Current project include anthologies on queer approaches to Tolkien and racisms and Tolkien as well as a planned monograph on how atheist, agnostic, and animist fans read Tolkien.

Dawn Walls-Thumma

Dawn Walls-Thumma is an independent scholar in Tolkien studies and fan studies. Her work focuses on Tolkien's use of pseudohistorical devices and the history and culture of the Tolkien fanfiction community and has been published in the Journal of Tolkien Research, Transformative Works and Cultures, and Mythprint, with chapters in the books Fandom: The Next Generation and Not the Fellowship: Dragons Welcome. Dawn is the founder of the Silmarillion Writers; Guild and the Tolkien Fanfiction Survey. In her non-Tolkien life, she teaches middle school humanities in a small Vermont village.

Joel Merriner

Joel Merriner is an Associate Lecturer in Art History at the University of Plymouth, where he teaches modules on art historical methodologies, visual culture, and the history of book illustration. His Ph.D. explored visual alterity within late Soviet-era Central and Eastern European illustrated translations of The Lord of the Rings. Joel is currently writing a monograph on Tolkien illustration in the Soviet Bloc. His latest research focuses on the global imaginary and the interconnected nature of Tolkien book illustration, fanart and film.

Danna Peterson-Deeprose

Danna Petersen-Deeprose studied literature at the graduate level at McGill University, where their research focused on representations of the sublime and the grotesque in literature. They now work as an editor at an academic press in Toronto, Canada, on the traditional territory of many nations including the Mississaugas of the Credit, the Anishnabeg, the Chippewa, the Haudenosaunee, and the Wendat peoples. They spend their time reading, writing fiction, and working with an online company to review and promote media by and about women and gender diverse people.

Sara Brown
Dr Sara Brown is Chair of the Language and Literature Faculty at Signum University, USA, where she has taught on courses with, amongst others, Corey Olsen, Verlyn Flieger, Dimitra Fimi, Robin Reid, Doug Anderson, Amy Sturgis, and John Garth. She completed her Ph.D. in Literature at Salford University in 2013; her thesis explores the way in which J.R.R. Tolkien was responding to the anxieties of modernity. Sara currently serves on the editorial board of *Mallorn*, the academic journal of the Tolkien Society, and is co-presenter on the Tolkien Experience Podcast, Rings of Power Wrap Up, and the Prancing Pony Podcast.

Nicholas Birns
Nicholas Birns teaches English at New York University and is the author of several articles and reviews on Tolkien that have appeared in *Mythlore*, *Tolkien Studies*, *Journal of Tolkien Research*, and *Journal of the Fantastic in the Arts*. He has published widely in literary studies. He is the author of *The Hyperlocal In Eighteenth and Nineteenth Century Literary Space* (Lexington), and is currently co-editing (with Louis Klee) *The Cambridge Companion to the Australian Novel*.

V. Elizabeth King
Elizabeth King, M.Ed is a PhD student in Human Development and Family Science at the University of Georgia. Elizabeth has a professional background in child welfare and her primary research is on traumatic stress, human rights, and child memory. As a lifelong Tolkien fan and enthusiast, Elizabeth's emerging interests in Tolkien scholarship center around defining and illuminating refugee and fostering narratives; complicating interpretations of perpetration and response to violence in the legendarium; and exploring textual and language-related evidence of colonization and resistance across cultures in Middle-earth. She has had a soft spot for wood-elves since childhood.

Clare Moore
Clare Moore is an independent scholar in the Washington D.C. area of the United States. Her research focuses on disability and gender in fantasy literature, specifically the works of J.R.R. Tolkien, and has appeared in *Mallorn*, *Journal of Tolkien Research*, *Mythlore*, and *The Polyphony*. Her essay 'A Song of Greater Power: Tolkien's Construction of Lúthien Tinúviel' won the Tolkien Society's 2022 award for Best Article.

Ingram Content Group UK Ltd.
Milton Keynes UK
UKHW050233270523
422386UK00013B/40

9 781915 556141